PRAISE FOR

EVEN IF

"Mitchel Lee, in his courageous authorial debut, shares what it's like to place faith in Christ amid hardship. For the follower of Jesus, *Even If* is not some bumper sticker to display but a daring commitment to live. It is a great book to read and a mantra for life."

—KYLE IDLEMAN, senior pastor of Southeast Christian Church and author of *Not a Fan* and *Don't Give Up*

"In the whirlwind of everyday life, where setbacks, unforeseen changes, and even heart-stricken grief are encountered often unexpectedly, we can easily be thrown off in our understanding of who God is and who we are. This book reminds us that the constancy of God's love for us and his strength are worthy anchors through the chaos."

—JENNY YANG, vice president for advocacy and policy at World Relief

"Suffering has caused more people to file for divorce from God than any other reason. *Even if* people—those who not only suffer but also proclaim in the midst of their suffering that *even if* they don't make it through, they'll still lean in and hold on to God—are rare today. I believe we will see more resilient people in the face of suffering because of this great book from my friend Mitchel Lee."

—BRYAN LORITTS, teaching pastor at the Summit Church and author of *The Dad Difference*

"Prophetic, pastoral, and personal in nature, *Even If* is a word for anyone in the valley, fire, or desert of spiritual life. Lee uniquely invites the reader to look for God in difficulty and, perhaps more importantly, determine to worship God, even when we can't find him. Ultimately, this is a book about real faith, deep faith, and anchored faith—a faith beyond private devotion and personal experience, inherited from ancient followers of God, ancient sufferers throughout Scripture, and those mighty saints who have gone before us."

—AUBREY SAMPSON, church planter and author of *The Louder Song* and *Known*

"*Even If* combines the insights of a seasoned biblical scholar with the empathy and honesty of a loving pastor. It's refreshingly honest, unexpectedly humorous, and enormously helpful. I have no doubt that it will help thousands of people navigate the pain and disappointment of life with a darker and more defiant faith."

➤ —PETE GREIG, founder of 24-7 Prayer International and author of *God on Mute*

"Whether we are walking through flames or living in the valley of the shadow of death, Mitchel Lee gives us hope and strengthens our resolve to stretch our faith in God, regardless of the circumstances. *Even If* is a book that will inspire your trust in God, who always comes through one way or another."

—DR. DAVID ANDERSON, author of the award-winning book *Gracism*

"I so relate to this book. Only those who have not lived enough years might miss the desperate need we have for the truth contained in these pages. If you find yourself as a valley dweller right now, or know someone who is, let Mitchell Lee be your personal guide to courage and freedom."

—RANDY FRAZEE, pastor and author of *His Mighty Strength*

"A well-written book full of pastoral wisdom and personal insights, the plot centers on the biblical confrontation between Daniel's three friends and Nebuchadnezzar, the king of Babylon. The author continues to circle back to this confrontation, making helpful application to difficult situations we face and what it means to live out an *even if* faith."

—DAVE MCDOWELL, pastor and author of *The Goodness of Affliction*

"Mitchel Lee is refreshingly real, deeply thoughtful, and biblically grounded. Whatever may come and wherever we may find ourselves, he points us with a pastor's heart toward life-giving hope and the powerful presence of God."

—DR. STEVE A. BROWN, president of Arrow Leadership
and author of *Jesus Centered*

EVEN IF

EVEN IF

TRUSTING GOD WHEN LIFE
DISAPPOINTS, OVERWHELMS, OR
JUST DOESN'T MAKE SENSE

MITCHEL LEE

MULTNOMAH

EVEN IF

Published in the United States by Multnomah, an imprint of Random House, a division of Penguin Random House LLC.

MULTNOMAH® and its mountain colophon are registered trademarks of Penguin Random House LLC.

LIBRARY OF CONGRESS CATALOGING-IN-PUBLICATION DATA
Names: Lee, Mitchel, author.
Title: Even if: trusting God when life disappoints, overwhelms, or just doesn't make sense / Mitchel Lee.
Description: Colorado Springs: Multnomah, 2021. | Includes bibliographical references.
Identifiers: LCCN 2020048236 | ISBN 9780593192528 (paperback) | ISBN 9780593192535 (ebook)
Subjects: LCSH: Trust in God—Christianity.
Classification: LCC BT135 .L375 2021 | DDC 231—dc23
LC record available at https://lccn.loc.gov/2020048236

Printed in the United States of America on acid-free paper

waterbrookmultnomah.com

1st Printing

First Edition

Interior book design by Caroline Cunningham.

SPECIAL SALES Most Multnomah books are available at special quantity discounts when purchased in bulk by corporations, organizations, and special-interest groups. Custom imprinting or excerpting can also be done to fit special needs. For information, please email specialmarketscms@penguinrandomhouse.com.

To a generation of immigrants whose *even if* faith made mine possible, Edward and Susie chief among them.

CONTENTS

WELCOME TO THE VALLEY

My graduation from seminary was supposed to be epic, the culmination of so much preparation and expectation. After three years of trekking back and forth between my home in Maryland and my seminary in North Carolina every Monday and Friday (a four-and-a-half-hour commute I wouldn't wish on my enemies), I looked forward to finally moving into the next chapter of my pastoral journey. I had worked my tail off during this season, leading a student ministry in Maryland while keeping up with my theological studies, and now I was ready to be fully unleashed into the world.

The March before graduation, the senior pastor of my church invited me into his office to talk. We hadn't talked like this before, so I should have known that something was up.

"Are you excited about graduation?" he probed.

"Absolutely. It'll be nice to be more present with the students and families I've been leading."

"I see. Well, I hear that you're interested in exploring more studies after your degree. Is that true?"

"That would be nice eventually. We'll have to see how it shapes up, though."

Insert awkward silence. "Hmm . . . I heard from someone that you were looking to move on, so we hired a new youth pastor. He'll start in June, so you're free to move on after graduation."

After the silence came an uppercut, a gut punch, devastation, and overall feelings of confusion and betrayal. *Why didn't he ask me about this rumor? What did I do wrong? How could he just hire my replacement? What about the students and families? The summer mission trips? What am I supposed to do after graduation?*

Just like that, the church I had served during my three years in seminary—and even more than that, the church I had grown up in, the one that had been my spiritual family for more than twenty years—had broken up with me.

And that wouldn't be the only heartbreak of spring 2002. I had been dating a young lady during seminary. Though we both had the long-term desire to get married, things weren't going well as time went on. On the weekend following my devastating conversation with my senior pastor, we reached a breaking point. Over lunch, she brought up the deep issues that were eroding our relationship. What ensued was a blame game that I had mastered. And because I am a pro when it comes to shifting responsibility and making the other person feel bad, the relationship was over before our entrées arrived.

I paid the check. We said our goodbyes, and I unknowingly walked into a wilderness that would last two years.

Rejected by my girlfriend and my home church, I limped to my seminary graduation, supported only by my immediate family and roommates. Imagine how difficult it was to sit through the commencement address with the customary triumphant charge "You can change the world!" transformed in the seminary setting into an ironic "*God* is sending you out to change the world!"

Sending me? I must have forgotten to pay my membership dues. While my fellow seminarians were taking on new pastorates or heading overseas to serve God, I was jobless, churchless, and alone. If God was sending our graduating class out, I felt stranded on the platform while the train was leaving the station.

The rest of the summer was a fog of blame and resentment. I bounced around various churches, worshipping in anonymity, taking the occasional speaking gig because I needed a paycheck. I was angry at God, disappointed that he would let my fledgling pastoral career disintegrate even before it really got started. This was not the plan.

Stunned by everything in my life crashing in such a sudden manner, I didn't have the strength or desire to connect meaning-fully with God. While I didn't abandon my faith in him, I kept him at a safe distance, going through the motions of what I thought I was supposed to do.

In need of a paycheck—and despite being in a place of des-peration and serious emotional unhealth—I accepted a pastoral position. Ignoring the pride and self-righteousness that had con-tributed to my exit from my home church, I chose to blame my surroundings instead of looking into my heart. Little did I know that the valley could actually get deeper. My term at the next church lasted exactly one year, ending with another curt termina-tion. I was devastated.

Upon my firing, I found myself managing my mom's deli, serv-ing breakfast and lunch Monday to Friday. I didn't want anything to do with pastoral ministry. Mind you, I hadn't given up on God or my relationship with him . . . I had given up on my calling to be a pastor. It was too hard, and there was too much pain involved. I would figure out other ways to serve God. At least, that's what I told myself.

Deep down, though, I believed my pride had disqualified me. I had hurt too many people. I had made too many mistakes, and

I could not expect any sort of blessing from the Lord. I had blown my chance. I lived for a year in the deep valley, trying to faithfully serve customers, helping my immigrant parents grow the family business.

With no aspirations and not believing that I deserved anything different, I stumbled upon the Puritan writer Richard Sibbes. His little book *The Bruised Reed* is a meditation on Isaiah 42:3: "A bruised reed he will not break, and a faintly burning wick he will not quench." My heart dared to wrestle with the thought of God's compassion for those who are bruised, discouraged, and disappointed—people whose flames are just barely burning. Did God really have compassion for someone like me? Could it be true that he wasn't done with me?

But what about the valley of disappointment I was in? My circumstances didn't proclaim that my life was blessed by or even in favor with God. It sure felt like he had snapped this reed and put out the faint flicker of my calling.

Providentially, God led me to a Sunday school story from my childhood. As I read Daniel 3, I was struck by the confidence of three young men with the names of a biblical tongue twister. Facing their own execution, they stood against the most powerful ruler in the world and declared their intention to remain true to their God: "If we are thrown into the blazing furnace, the God we serve is able to deliver us from it, and he will deliver us from Your Majesty's hand. *But even if* he does not, we want you to know, Your Majesty, that we will not serve your gods or worship the image of gold you have set up" (verses 17–18, NIV, emphasis added).

Even if . . . The words seared into my consciousness, inviting me to get up and continue walking with God *even if* I felt alone, *even if* I was disqualified, *even if* I might be forgotten. As I studied the passage, I realized that this declaration wasn't unique to these three men. The *even if* declaration resonated through the lives of countless biblical witnesses. I couldn't unsee it—with each biblical account, God was forming me. With trembling heart and grace-shaped resolve, I declared, *"Even if* I never pastor a church or preach again, I will worship you, God. You've done enough. You're worthy. My life belongs to you."

I don't know when I actually ascended out of the valley. I don't even know whether I ascended or whether the valley floor was somehow raised. I do know that my faith and walk with God have never been the same. This declaration continues to define my life and ministry. As I have experienced many valleys since, I have been learning fresh ways to say *even if*—to declare my commitment to worship a God who may not act in the ways I desire but always acts in ways that are good.

This is a book about how to worship God in the valley. This is a book for the strugglers, the ones who are trying to make sense of lives that haven't gone the way they hoped. This is a call to the hopeful realists, those who are holding on to faith, if even by the barest of threads.

It's not about escaping the valley. Believe me, I wish I could give you an instruction manual to avoid the valley. I wish I could give you a magical incantation that would make faith come alive, explain every disappointment, and connect all the dots for you. All I have for you is what God has taught me in the many valleys I've lived in, as well as those I've walked through with other people.

Whatever brought you here—be it desperation or just reluctant curiosity—we have a common experience: the damp, shadowy, chilling depths of the valley, that place of forgottenness and isolation. For some it can last for a season, but for others it can be the defining theme of their lives. Sometimes we can be in a valley for so long that it becomes the norm, making anything else seem like a celestial peak.

You might find yourself in a valley right now. You want to call it quits. You're wondering how much more you can endure or how much more you have left to give. The loss of a job, the test results that came back positive, the accident you never anticipated, the ministry that crashed, the loss of a child, the betrayal of a friend, the disappointment of dreams unfulfilled, a pandemic—all these can leave us gasping for air, feeling as though we're surrounded with no hope of rescue. Valley life.

Some people are absolutely undone in the valley. They get punched in the gut and never get back up. Jaded and bitter, they resent not only their own circumstances but also the perceived happiness of all those on the cliffs above them. They respond by protecting themselves with layers of defensive coping strategies. They stop taking risks. They vow to order their lives so as to control every detail. No one and nothing will ever hurt them again.

Still, where many throw in the towel, others find renewed life. Author David Brooks described them as "second-mountain people."[1] They are the ones who are thrust into the valley and experience a second birth. The suffering of the valley leads to wisdom, which then leads to service. The wilderness breaks them in an important, maturing way. They find a new level of resolve, a deep reservoir of strength that they didn't know existed. They transcend their egos. Faith becomes a lifeline. Their relationships with God plumb new depths of intimacy. Disappointment and its resulting frustration and confusion become the fertilizer (and we all know where fertilizer comes from) for a deep faith that worships God no matter what. The wilderness becomes the birthplace of devotion.

Jesus told his disciples, "I came that they may have life and have it abundantly" (John 10:10). I believe that can be true for life in the valley. God can give you abundant life there when you make your own *even if* declaration. Whatever or whoever pushed you into the valley, that is not the end of your story. The bold, faith-filled, and defiant resolution of three young men in Daniel 3 can free you to hope and trust God, no matter the circumstances. In other words, disappointments and setbacks don't have to define us. They might explain us—our personalities, our quirkiness, and our reflexive instincts—but they don't have to define us.

In order to experience the *even if* life, there's work to do. It won't be easy. You may have to retrace paths that you would rather forget. God may ask you to revisit painful places, remember difficult people, or even walk along the rocky shores that shipwrecked your expectations and dreams. At some point, you'll wonder whether it's worth it. The fear and heartache can be too much. I'm praying for your willingness and courage to remember who God is, to praise him in *all* circumstances, and to believe that he has not forgotten you. *Even if.*

We'll unpack this declaration in several phases. First we'll look at what it actually is. We'll examine the story of Shadrach, Meshach, and Abednego in Daniel 3 and see how unthinkable their *even if* declaration actually is. Then we'll break down the declaration into its two basic parts.

With the basic components of the *even if* declaration before us, we'll uncover the *counter ifs* that threaten to undo our devotion. The unpredictability of life has a way of subtly convincing us that we have to fend for ourselves. We develop defense mechanisms that can accommodate faith while slowly distorting it. We write counterfeit declarations that keep us stuck, unable to move forward in our walks with God. Part of the work in declaring your own *even if* will be to recognize the *counter ifs* that we've adopted and to begin surrendering them to God.

Finally, we'll think about how to live the *even if* life . . . what it means for our daily habits and attitudes, as well as some *even if* steps we can take today. The end goal of it all is to live courageously with conviction and faith in the power and goodness of a God who promises to be with us no matter where life takes us. And his promise, my friend, can make all the difference.

PART 1

SOMEWHERE BEYOND THE SEA

In May 1940, the German war machine advanced through France, taking city after city. With each successive German victory, weary and defeated Allied forces made up of British, French, and Belgian soldiers retreated like a trail of ants toward the town of Dunkirk on the northwest coast of France. Over three hundred thousand troops eventually assembled along the twenty-seven-mile stretch from Dunkirk to the northern town of Ostend, awaiting evacuation or capture. The British citizenry watched helplessly from across the English Channel, and as the troops amassed, their morale deflated.

British military leaders spent sleepless nights trying to find a way to rescue their stranded soldiers. Operation Dynamo, as it was called, was a bold and desperate operation dependent on weather, military tactics, and raw luck. Expectations were low. Winston Churchill believed that rescuing just fifteen thousand troops would be an act of divine intervention.

In a series of now-famous radio messages, King George VI overcame his stuttering to summon his people's resolve and endurance. Legend has it that, in response to one of King George's messages, the stranded British army sent a three-word message across the

English Channel: "And if not"[1]—a reference to the story of the three young men who defied the king of Babylon. The intent of the message was that *even if* they were not rescued, they would not bow to Germany.

The three-word message reinvigorated the people. Citizens stepped up to try to shuttle as many soldiers as they could take, in as many trips as necessary. From commercial fishing ships to recreational yachts, everyone who could carry even a few soldiers braved waters infested by U-boats and sea mines. Such was the urgency that some ships embarked without sea charts or maps. The entire country rallied together.

"The miracle of Dunkirk" was exactly that.[2] All told, over 338,000 troops were evacuated in ten days. Operation Dynamo stands out as one of the most incredible operations in military history. All catalyzed by a simple message: *even if.*°

Words have power. They can give life or death. You can remember the words spoken to you at just the right time, words that made the difference between continuing and giving up. Sometimes just a few words can alter the trajectory of a nation. (Think, "I have a dream . . .")[3]

A simple declaration saved hundreds of thousands of lives and ultimately a continent. The same words that ignited the resilience of a nation can revive your soul: *even if.*

In order to unleash the power of this concept, we have to understand it. In this first part, we'll take a closer look at the biblical story. Later we'll break down the *even if* declaration into its two parts: trusting the goodness of God and resolving to worship him.

° The exact words of the message were "And if not . . ." The NIV renders the phrase "Even if"—this was the translation I was reading at the time I described earlier.

1

Out of the Fire . . . or into It?

At an early age, I was told, "God loves you and has a wonderful plan for your life." It was the opening line of a greater invitation to surrender my life to Jesus and invite him into my heart. If I did, the promise went on, "God will forgive you and lead you in ways you could never imagine." While I certainly have no regrets about saying yes to that invitation years ago, I have come to realize that I made some serious assumptions about what God was inviting me into—and you know what happens when we assume.

Maybe I was reading between the lines. I assumed that the fruit of surrendering to God's wonderful plan was a life with less pain and no confusion. I reasoned that since I trusted him, I could not be disappointed or feel uncertain. After all, God would always be with me. It was a simple formula: my trust + his plan = smooth sailing.

I do the trusting, he does the planning, and we're all good.

It's okay if you're shaking your head, thinking, *How naive.* Life has a way of exposing our naivete. For me, all it took was getting picked on, seasons of intense loneliness, watching my parents' crazy fights, and experiencing financial hardships to realize that God's plan didn't equal smooth sailing at all.

As my relationship with God deepened, I came to realize that a trouble-free life is never part of the promise. In fact, the Scriptures guarantee the opposite.

We will have hardships—physical pain, sorrow, disappointment, and sometimes just general confusion. You have had your own tough experiences. Perhaps you are in one right now. Life has not gone the way you wanted. You are disillusioned. Hurt. Maybe just plain stuck while everyone else seems to be moving forward just fine. You might be none of those things, but living in a world shaped by COVID-19 has caused you to question the things that, until now, you thought were certain.

While the season you've come through or are in right now might have been a surprise to you, it wasn't a surprise to Jesus. In his last lengthy talk with his disciples, just before he was betrayed and crucified, Jesus made a promise: "I have said these things to you, that in me you may have peace. In the world you will have tribulation. But take heart; I have overcome the world" (John 16:33). Did you see the two parts to it? He guaranteed the trouble just as he guaranteed *his presence.*

The disciples were going to face all kinds of opposition from the world, and so are we. They would be afflicted, and so will we. He called them to be strengthened in their resolve—that is what "take heart" means—because he has overcome the world. The one who has overcome the world would be with them. Jesus called for trust in the midst of trouble.

If you're like me, you love to believe in the certainty of his presence but not necessarily the certainty of trouble. Can't we just have his presence without the problems? I think, *I could learn to trust without the trouble. I'm a really quick learner. Just give me the good stuff, and I'll trust you! I promise.*

My unwillingness to accept the promise of trouble makes me

wonder, *Have I really outgrown my childhood assumptions about what it means to trust in God?* I hate to admit that the formula still shapes my outlook in subtle ways. Life's difficulties expose them. And with every twist and turn, every time I feel shocked when life knocks me upside the head yet again, I have the opportunity to revisit what my faith means for living in this broken world.

I suppose being shocked is better than the tragic alternative—growing bitter and cynical to the point where we're suspicious if life goes smoothly. I have met people like that. The curmudgeon who refuses to receive any help from anyone. The friend who thinks that his failures are everyone's fault but his own. The boss who feels that everyone is out for her job, whose insecurity will never let her apologize. The embittered family member who feels as though the world owes him something.

Pessimism and distrust have a way of sucking the life out of every moment. Like people wearing those high-tech noise-canceling headphones, some hear only one soundtrack to life. They are always looking for the angle or expecting the other shoe to drop. Gratitude goes extinct because they suspect there is always a catch—some sort of karmic retribution that will make sure they end up paying for whatever moment of peace or joy might have come their way.

Cynics didn't get that way overnight. They faced trouble and disappointment enough times to harden their hearts. At one time, they were hopeful. After they got knocked to the mat too many times, their best defense was to forsake the expectation that life would get any better. They just stopped hoping. They simply stopped trying. They chose bitterness because it was at least more predictable than dashed expectations.

IS THAT ALL THERE IS?

Are these your only options? Continually getting floored by the frustrations of life or growing cynical and expecting nothing but disappointment? I believe that God offers you more—a third option, to trust him even when life is hard. The relationship he invites you to does not require nice weather to flourish. In fact, that is why God can deepen your faith even when the storms of life upend your dreams, plans, and expectations. No matter what life has thrown at you, it is possible not only to endure but even to move forward, trusting God for whatever comes next.

Have you ever seen glimpses of this kind of faith in other people? In a cancer patient who seems to draw on a reservoir of strength that you wish could be bottled and shared. Perhaps in a senior who has lived through incredibly hard times yet exudes the gentleness and sweetness of a child. I have been warmed by the resilience and never-give-up determination of colleagues who have devoted many years to fighting for the forgotten and overlooked. People like that are our heroes. We want to be like them.

And I believe we can. There are no shortcuts, though. The kind of faith I am describing forms as we cling to Jesus's presence in hardships. And to cling to Jesus in trouble means *it will take trouble.* Another way to say it is that difficulties can therefore be redemptive. And "lucky" for you and me, we don't have to manufacture the trouble. Life will bring it.

The life-transforming truth is that we are left not at the mercy of our situations but rather at the mercy of a loving God who leads us and does have wonderful plans for us. Seeing him in the midst of the trouble will take some shifting of our perspectives, some personal reflection, and a lot of courage.

We will need to remind ourselves over and over who God is and what he has done for us. And when we do, we will develop a reflex-like disposition for our faith that informs how we respond to life's situations—good or bad.

The kind of faith I am describing expresses itself in . . .

- resolve to trust God in ways that we never thought possible
- endurance amid difficulties that we didn't know we had strength for
- peace and hope that are so otherworldly they can bless and transform others

This kind of faith can flow from a simple but powerful declaration, one that catalyzed my own transformation and continues to this day. I was in the midst of a dark wilderness season, stuck and alone. Yet in the middle of my valley, God spoke two life-giving words that resurrected me. Two words from a children's Sunday school story.

FAITH THROUGH FLAMES

The first time I heard the story of Daniel, I wasn't really paying attention . . . until our Sunday school teacher bribed us with candy if we would only sit still long enough for her to get through the lesson. She used a black flannelgraph board and cutout pictures to tell us about Daniel and his three friends in Babylon. Back then, it was cutting-edge technology for children's ministry, an analog version of PowerPoint. She told us the story of three young men in Babylon who boldly stood firm in their faith against a powerful king. They were miraculously delivered from a fiery furnace because they trusted God. She then asked, "Who will stand up for Jesus like Shadrach, Meshach, and Abednego?"

One by one, we stood and proclaimed our allegiance to God. "I will trust God no matter what kind of fire comes!" we all shouted. Then we received our Jolly Rancher reward. Simple enough. The lasting image of this story became for me three flame-retardant young men miraculously standing alongside Jesus—a fireproof Savior for any situation. The story stuck.

The Scriptures are imaginative and simple enough to nurture the faith of a young child. But they also have a depth that grows to accommodate what David Brooks observed: "These stories kept coming back, but they changed, as if re-formed by the alchemy of time. They grew bigger and deeper, more fantastical and more astonishing."[1]

Over the years, through encountering my own fiery furnaces, that Sunday school story has grown bigger and deeper for me. As I look more closely, imagining the emotions and tensions embedded in the drama of Daniel 3, the response of the three young men is as surprising as the miraculous deliverance from the fire. Let me explain.

Nebuchadnezzar was the king of Babylon, the most powerful man on the planet. He had conquered every rival power, including the small province of Judah.* Not even the previous superpower, Assyria, could conquer Jerusalem. But the Babylonians marched in, laid siege, took over the city, and forcibly removed the people of God from their land.

Nebuchadnezzar had the entire world at his fingertips, but he desired more acclaim. So he came up with a great idea: "Since I'm the greatest, why not have everyone acknowledge that I'm the greatest?" He built a huge statue, summoned all the officials of the empire, and, on the day of the statue's dedication, played his Nebuchadnezzar-ian theme song so everyone could bow down to it. I imagine that it was quite a demonstration of absolute rule, a choreographed ritual of worship and nationalistic loyalty.

Everything was going according to plan. Nebuchadnezzar was

---

* Actually, unbeknownst to Nebuchadnezzar, God handed Judah over to him because of their continuing rebellion and unfaithfulness.

excited to see the reflection of his own worth in his prostrate subjects. Except . . . three high-ranking officials in his own province—Shadrach, Meshach, and Abednego—refused to bow! To add insult to treachery, these were men whom he himself had appointed, men from a vanquished city called Jerusalem.

In a furious rage, the king summoned them to the site of the fiery furnace to explain themselves. How dare his own officials ignore his decree? Maybe there was some sort of misunderstanding. These Babylonian officials were, after all, not from around there. Perhaps something got lost in translation.

The king sought confirmation: "Is it true, O Shadrach, Meshach, and Abednego, that you do not serve my gods or worship the golden image that I have set up?" (Daniel 3:14).

By not bowing down, these three officials refused to engage in Babylonian-sanctioned worship. It was not just a rejection of Babylonian culture or a display of personal preferences. It was an act of treason against the king.

Nebuchadnezzar threatened, *"If you are ready,* when the music plays, you will bow down and worship the image I have made. *And if not,* you will immediately be cast into the midst of a fiery furnace" (see verse 15).

Nebuchadnezzar finished his threat with a rhetorical question just to make sure these young officials understood the situation they were in: "And who is the god who will deliver you out of my hands?" (verse 15). In other words, "If you refuse me, who can save you?" The most powerful man on the planet stated his case, asserted his authority, and surely expected contrition and fealty.

The king's straightforward threat is what makes the response of the young men so stunning. With equal parts defiance and matter-of-fact explanation, they declared that they didn't even really need to answer the king in this matter. The answer to his question was so obvious, they didn't even think it warranted an answer.

"If this happens, our God whom we serve is able to deliver us from the fiery furnace, and he can save us from your hand. *And if not,* you need to know we won't serve your gods or worship this image" (see verses 17–18).

Nebuchadnezzar's ultimatum was met with an equally resolute declaration: *"Even if* God does not deliver us, we won't worship any other or bow down to you." They weren't oblivious to the threat before them. This wasn't naive optimism or blind faith. With the heat of a fire drying out their eyes, they refused the king.

The two parts of their response to the king make up one of the most powerful declarations in the Bible. They declared . . .

1. their confidence in a good God who was able to deliver them
2. their resolve to worship him *even if* he didn't

In other words, the God whom they served, the God of the Bible, is more powerful than the king they stood before. Their God could override the king's decree and neutralize his threats. "My God is bigger than your god." You probably expected as much from a Bible story. Faith against the odds.

But this is where it takes an unexpected twist. They went on to declare not only that God could save them but also that *even if* their all-powerful God chose not to demonstrate his power to save (seemingly giving Nebuchadnezzar the win), they would not give their loyalty to another. Their allegiance belonged to God regardless of how he chose to act or not act on their behalf. And consequently, no matter how much the king huffed and puffed, they would not give their loyalty to him.

Even if. These are the two words that can transform your expectations and strengthen your faith. The *even if* declaration can help you stand before a fire and trust God even when the outcome is not yet decided. It refuses to succumb to the current pressure or disappointment, and in that sense, it is a surprising declaration in trouble. It expresses confidence and resolve when all the conditions seem to warrant doubt and compromise.

The *even if* declaration is all the more surprising when we consider how these *even if* declarers ended up in Babylon in the first place.

A LONG WAY FROM HOME

Though the warnings had come for a while now, no one took them seriously. Jeremiah's anti-nationalistic, doom-and-gloom prophecies were dismissed by counterprophets, and their logic seemed more compelling. No way would the city of God, the very place where God had made his dwelling, fall to an enemy. God would never forsake his people, despite their idolatrous tendencies and unfaithfulness.

Even as news began to flow from the north about a new threat—an army from the faraway land of Babylon—life (and unfaithfulness to God) went on. Then one day, a shadow began to grow on the horizon of the Judean wilderness. Dots became horses and chariots. Dust clouds rose as a war machine advanced toward their city.

False prophets stubbornly refuted what everyone was seeing: Jeremiah's message coming true. They reassured the people that God would always uphold the glory of his name by preserving his city. All this talk about God handing over his people for judgment and exile was just a scare tactic. Babylon would be turned back just as previous would-be invaders had been.

Then the city fell. The temple was looted. Jehoiachin the king, the son of Jehoiakim, captured. Per the usual Babylonian policy, all the promising youth, including Daniel and his three friends, Shadrach, Meshach, and Abednego, were trafficked to Babylon to be acculturated and then assimilated into the Babylonian Empire. Their names were changed, and they were taught a new language, (re)educated, and given positions in government.

And all the while, the prophecies of the now-vindicated Jeremiah echoed: "Don't count on returning to Jerusalem. Make your home in Babylon. It's gonna be a while."

Fast-forward to where Shadrach, Meshach, and Abednego (Daniel was up to some other defiance elsewhere) stood before their captor and declared their confidence in their God.

How could these men continue to trust in God's power to deliver when he had not in the past? How could they declare their faith with such conviction when they were facing the very king who had brought about Jerusalem's downfall? It would be understandable if they gave up on the God who had seemingly given up on them.

This is the challenge that everyone who trusts in God will face. Expectations go unmet. Promises go unkept. Blessings run dry. Prayers go unanswered. Our hearts get broken.

People respond to this challenge in various ways. Some defiantly recant their faith, emotionally unable to worship a God who would abandon them. The silence of God—both in word and in action—discourages them to the point of numbness. In the words of Fleming Rutledge, "Even God's wrath would be preferable to God's absence."[2] People suffering like that abandon God and look to other sources of strength: their own ability, others around them, or whatever would-be savior looks plausible.

Others tame their faith while continuing to go through the motions. Instead of explicit rejection, quiet resignation sets in. While not abandoning God altogether, they develop an arms-length distance from him. They might acknowledge him by dropping in on weekly worship gatherings or staying in relationship with other Christians, but they functionally act like their own god. They follow God as long as they don't have to depend on him for anything of real importance. They have come to believe that it just works better this way.

Yet Shadrach, Meshach, and Abednego chose another way. They chose to trust in God not for the benefits they received but because of who he is and what he is able to do. Tim Keller observed the almost-paradoxical nature of their declaration.[3] They had faith in God's ability to save but were willing to admit the possibility of not being delivered. At first glance, it might seem contradictory. How can you trust God and still be open to the possibility that he might not do what you want? But that's exactly the point—a robust faith believes God so deeply that even if he doesn't do what you think he should, you trust that he is working for your good. This is the kind of faith from which an *even if* declaration arises.

FAITH THAT'S BIGGER THAN ME

I'm not very handy. While I can follow directions and build IKEA furniture with the best of them, beyond that I am not a craftsman. It usually takes me several tries to hang a picture straight. Forget about anything involving electricity or plumbing. I have, however, built other kinds of things: ministries, teams, and organizations. I know that if you're going to build something well (whether it's a house or a church), a solid foundation is essential.

The same holds true for our faith. Jesus gave an entire parable about building our lives on a solid foundation (Luke 6:46–49). Someone who comes to Jesus, hears his words, and does them is like a person building a house on solid rock. When storms come, the house will stand. Pretty straightforward stuff.

I wonder, though, whether we subtly depart from this belief. Especially in our day of self-help, when pursuing our own happiness is the highest objective, building our faith on Jesus can be thought of as a subjective practice: just Jesus, self, and a cup of coffee with the latest worship album. We can think we're building a foundation on Jesus, but this kind of faith has an inherent weakness. It will be only as strong as our own experiences of him.

Shadrach, Meshach, and Abednego demonstrated a faith informed by more than just their personal stories. Their devotion flowed from a deeper spring than the surface streams of their circumstances. That is what gave them confidence to trust God in the face of the fire. Their faith was built on the work of God in ages past.

Maybe they recalled the way God had delivered their people from Egypt at the Exodus and provided for them in the wilderness. And he had delivered a previous generation from the mighty Assyrians. Time and time again, they had heard about God's miraculous deliverance and his faithful, covenant-keeping love.

All these remembrances formed a larger body of work demonstrating God's character and power, a body of work that encompassed much more than their lives. It was enough to warrant their confident devotion even if they hadn't personally experienced his deliverance.

This is where the *even if* declaration finds its foundation: in the objective, historical testimony of Scripture and saints of old. What Shadrach, Meshach, and Abednego built on is available to you too. Your faith is much more than just private devotion, a set of personal values or experiences that holds true only for you. God has been at work throughout human history, providing for and leading men and women in profound and powerful ways. His fingerprints are everywhere, even in the darkest of times. Remembering this can make all the difference in whom we know God to be . . . especially when facing the fire.

Standing before the most powerful human being on the planet, eyes squinting from stinging sweat, faces seared by the raging heat of the furnace, Shadrach, Meshach, and Abednego remained confident. God could save them from the fire because he had saved past generations. Because he is all powerful, he was able to save them. And even if he chose not to, he was worthy of their worship.

Their confidence in God was extraordinary, but their circumstances were not any more exceptional than what we face today. In a world of increasing hostilities and political tensions, coronaviruses, cancer, family breakdowns, persecution, terrorist attacks, and armed conflicts, can we look out on the world we live in and have this same confidence in our God's ability to deliver? What's the larger body of work that your faith is built on? Is God worthy of your worship?

THE *EVEN IF* OUTCOME

Nebuchadnezzar reacted with fury over their brazen defiance. I can empathize. If my own children responded that way, it wouldn't end well. Daniel 3 says that "the expression of his face was changed against Shadrach, Meshach, and Abednego" (verse 19). Whatever mercy or empathy the king had sought to extend now evaporated. He ordered the furnace heated up seven times hotter than usual. The furnace was so hot that even the guards whose duty it was to throw them in died in the act. As tempered as the three young men's collective response seems, the king's retaliation was disproportionately ablaze with fury. He wanted them to hurt, and he didn't care whom he hurt in the process.

The *even if* declaration didn't soften the circumstances; it intensified them. An *even if* declaration isn't some sort of magical charm that clears the path in front of us. It didn't work that way for Shadrach, Meshach, and Abednego. They declared their trust in God's power and goodness and their resolve to worship him alone, but that declaration didn't give them an out. Instead, it literally increased the heat. The choice to trust and worship their God became a confrontation. A would-be god versus the true and living One. There's no middle ground or compromise possible here, no playing both sides. Bow or burn.

How did the story turn out? God did indeed save. Nebuchadnezzar saw a fourth person in the fire, one "like a son of the gods" (verse 25). This divine figure stood with the three men and protected them such that not even their clothes were singed nor did they smell of smoke. These would-be burnt offerings experienced what scholars call a theophany—a manifestation of God. In that way, the young men got more than deliverance. They got God's very presence.

The king accepted his place. He summarily declared, "Blessed be the God of Shadrach, Meshach, and Abednego, who has sent his angel and delivered his servants, who trusted in him, and set aside the king's command, and yielded up their bodies rather than serve and worship any god except their own God" (verse 28).

Nebuchadnezzar's blessing offers two important observations. First, the most powerful man on the planet acknowledged the saving power of someone greater. God had indeed delivered his servants, answering the earlier question the king posed: "Who is the god who will deliver you out of my hands?" (verse 15). Shadrach, Meshach, and Abednego's confident declaration— "Our God whom we serve is able to deliver us from the burning fiery furnace, and he will deliver us out of your hand, O king" (verse 17)—was proved true.

Second, the king commended their devotion and commitment to the God who could deliver. The acknowledgment is an important one. Nebuchadnezzar saw that the young men's defiance wasn't just stubbornness or a nihilistic resignation to whatever fate might bring. Nor was it the expression of a naive, triumphalist faith that refused to accept the possibility of death. No, they were willing to die, to yield their own bodies rather than serve any other. In ironic fashion, the king was the one to explain the true motivation behind their actions. Their refusal to bow down flowed from a greater devotion to a greater God.

Nebuchadnezzar then issued an empire-wide declaration. No one in the empire was to speak anything against the God of Shadrach, Meshach, and Abednego, because there is no other God who could rescue *in this way*. And what way is this?

God could have kept the young men from the fire in any number of miraculous ways. He could have caused the fire to go out. He could have changed Nebuchadnezzar's mind. If he could make wet wood catch fire in the case of Elijah's confrontation with the prophets of Baal (1 Kings 18), surely he could have prevented the fire from burning. But the three young men weren't spared from the furnace. God allowed them to be cast into it. Rather than changing the circumstances, God made his presence known in and through them. Remember Jesus's promise? Presence in trouble.

This is often how God works. In fact, in another part of Scripture, God sent the prophet Isaiah to foretell Israel's exile and how he would deliver them:

> When you pass through the waters, I will be with you;
> and through the rivers, they shall not overwhelm you;
> when you walk through fire you shall not be burned,
> and the flame shall not consume you. (43:2)

It doesn't say *if* you walk through the fire but *when*. And when you're in the fire, you won't be burned. You won't be consumed.

God sometimes allows us to go through the fire. When we are faced with difficulties or uncertainties—the fires of life—our instinctive response is to do what we can to change the circumstances. We ask God to put out the fire. Or at least turn down the heat. Change the king's mind. Shut the furnace door. Show that you're God. How many times have I operated from the belief that what I needed most was a changed situation rather than more of God in the midst of the situation?

As an example of how easy it is to think this way, think about when you last talked through a problem with someone. Chances are that most of the advice you were given had to do with how to change your situation. Maybe the person suggested you cut off the relationship, removing yourself from the negativity. Perhaps he or she pointed out what you needed to do differently. Little of the advice we receive has to do with enduring.

God allows us to walk through the fire so that we might experience his presence, not just his power. By being with us in the trouble, he shows us that he cares for us, not as a genie who makes life trouble-free but as the God who loves us and calls us into relationship with him.

Even in the toughest circumstances, we have the opportunity to declare *even if*—holding in one hand our confidence in a God who can save and in the other our resolve that *even if* he does not, we will still worship him.

Even if is a declaration of both faith and uncertainty—a way to express our faith and hope in a God who cares about our lives in the tension of the unpredictable, difficult world we live in. And after all is said and done, while God might not always change our circumstances, his presence will change us in the fire.

No other God rescues in this way, and it isn't true just of a fiery furnace in Babylon. God rescued all of humanity, not just three young men. And look at how he did it: God came to us as Immanuel, which literally means "God with us." God left the glory of heaven, put on flesh, and lived among us. He experienced the pain and suffering of this world, and he died for the sins that messed everything up in the first place.

In this way, Jesus came and walked into the furnace not just with us but for us. He chose to be forsaken in the furnace of his sufferings so that we might be forgiven. And after his resurrection, just before he ascended to the Father, he promised, "Behold, I am with you always, to the end of the age" (Matthew 28:20). That means, in every valley, in every fire, we can declare our *even if* with confidence in the God who delivers *even if* it's in ways that we could not imagine.

That's what faith in God gives us. The possibility and opportunity for transformation no matter where we are. Before we look at how to live out this faith in concrete steps, let's consider in a little more detail the two parts of the *even if* declaration.

Goodness in the Deep End of the Pool

My Korean immigrant parents were both small-business owners. Days off didn't come often, so I was surprised when one day in the summer just before my sixth birthday, my dad decided not to open his store.

"Let's go swimming today," he announced.

"Yes! But I don't know how to swim, Dad."

"That's okay. This is the perfect chance for me to teach you," he offered with enough confidence for both of us.

My mom packed gear for the day—the usual assortment of towels, sunscreen, and, of course, an incredible feast of a lunch and enough snacks to outlast a nuclear apocalypse. Such were the perks of owning your own carryout deli, I suppose.

These were the days before flotation devices were expected parts of child aquatic wear. Puddle Jumper life vests had not yet been invented, and the most common apparatus for child water safety was an inflatable water wing that never quite fit around your upper arm (and which, unfortunately, sometimes served only as a bobber to locate where your face was actually submerged). Still, those sorts of devices were for overcautious people. My parents figured that if they were going to be that scared, they probably shouldn't be going into the water in the first place.

With nothing but the swim trunks I was wearing for a life preserver, I was so excited to get my first real swim lesson. My father was a good swimmer—at least, I tell myself that today. We arrived at the pool, and while my parents were getting us stationed for the day, I was already knee deep in the kids' end, splashing around and dreaming of the ways that I was going to conquer and explore this rectangular playground.

After probably a hundred "Can we swim now?" inquiries, my father led me by the hand deeper into the pool. Like the ring announcer before a WWE match, he asked, "Are you ready to swim?" Before I could even say yes—and as if he assumed my answer—he launched me into the air.

Just like every other part of my upbringing, my dad's swim school was founded on the immigrant philosophy of "sink or swim"—only this time literally. I didn't even have time to scream. Some combination of my instinct to survive and my initial shock numbed any sort of vocal cry as I hit the water and immediately began thrashing for my life.

After drinking a gallon of chlorinated water, I felt two arms pull me up. I coughed up enough water to be able to talk and let out a cry of shock and confusion between convulsive breaths.

"Why did you throw me? Don't—"

Before I could finish the sentence, he proceeded to cast me away from him just far enough that I had to paddle back toward him. Actually, *paddle* is way too graceful a term to describe what I was doing. It was more like thrashing and flailing in a direction.

We were too far into the pool for me to find refuge on its walls. So we repeated our little exchange over and over again. I would make my way toward him, or he would pick me up if I was sinking. Somehow, each time he would overcome my death grip on his body and fling me yet again. My fingernails tattooed a desperate pattern of red tracks all over his body, henna-like signs of my failed attempts to hold on for dear life.

I ended up learning how to swim that day. I also learned how to drink lots of pool water and not throw up. I obviously didn't die. But in the midst of it, I really believed I was going to. You have no ability to logically reason or think clearly when the waters are over your head.

During my first and only class in immigrant swim school, I actually believed that my father—the man who had literally crossed an ocean in order to give me a better life—was going to let me die in that small swimming pool. I forgot who he was and what he had done. I even forgot that my mom was watching from her poolside lounger. (Her passive role in my memory is a whole other topic.)

After having kids of my own, I see how unfounded my fears were. Whether they're refusing to eat a delectable but visually unappealing dish or rebelling against going to bed when it's obvious they're way past a sane level of tired, even the youngest of my children repeatedly demonstrates the basic instinct of the human heart to look out for number one.

When a threat comes, have you ever noticed how easy it is to distrust the very people who have given you every reason to put your fate in their hands? Parents, siblings, BFFs, doctors, coaches, teachers—these are people we usually trust and depend on. But sometimes in moments of hardship or uncertainty, we can forget their body of work—character, faithfulness, competence—and we fend for ourselves.

When we are sinking in deep waters or facing the fire of life, a kind of self-preserving amnesia can also infect our faith. The obstacle or opponent in front of us can cause us to forget who God is because we're just trying to survive. And when we forget who

God is, whatever we are facing appears even more menacing. Despair and distrust set in.

In those times, we must remember who God is, and who we are as a result. The *even if* declaration helps us do this by beginning with the call to remember the true character and ability of our heavenly Father. Reviewing Daniel 3:17–18, the two parts of the *even if* declaration are . . .

1. confidence in a good God who is able to deliver
2. resolve to worship him *even if* he doesn't

Before the most powerful man on the planet, Shadrach, Meshach, and Abednego declared their trust in God. Even when facing a raging fire, they didn't succumb to instinctive amnesia. They declared that God was able to deliver. Beneath their trust in God's ability, though, was a deeper trust in God's character. He is a good God.

What does it mean to say "God is good"? If you grew up in church, you know that Christians overuse lots of phrases to the point of not being sure what exactly they mean. Often, when you hear "God is good," someone will, in call-and-response fashion, shout "All the time!" I believe that to be true, but we need to unpack what exactly God's goodness means in the face of the fire.

LET'S PLAY WORD ASSOCIATION

My family loves to play a word game where we choose a category, then take turns naming various subjects that make up that category. Sometimes to make it harder, we play a version where we have to name them alphabetically. Lately the category of choice has been Marvel characters. So it might go like this:

"Ant-Man."

Followed by "Black Panther."

Then "Captain America."

"Daredevil." And so on.

(I just wrote that off the top of my head. Impressed?)

Having confidence in the goodness of God is like a faith-fueled word-association exercise. We have to nuance how God demonstrates his goodness. In fact, our faith deepens as we learn by both experience and study what his goodness entails. Play along with me. God is the category. Now how many of his attributes can we name? How are those attributes expressions of his goodness? Bonus points if you can do it alphabetically. Let's try: God's aseity,° beauty, compassion, determination . . . and so on.

More than just theological jargon, these qualities make up your understanding of who God is, and the implications are enormous. A. W. Tozer described it best in the opening line of his work *The Knowledge of the Holy:* "What comes into our minds when we think about God is the most important thing about us."[1] In other words, whom you believe God to be will determine how you respond to every situation in life, whether the mountaintops, the valleys, or the flatlands in between. Ask yourself, in the midst of whatever you are facing right now, *Who is God? Is he good?*

What does *good* even mean? The word is thrown around to mean a lot of things today. We use it to describe a meal or a movie, a lover or an experience. It shows up as the generic response when you ask your kid, "How was school today?" or when you ask a friend, "How was your vacation?" If the only response is "Good," we might think he or she had an indifferent experience, is unwilling to talk about it, or is trying to gloss over what was actually a difficult time.

° God's aseity has to do with the fact that God exists in and of himself. He is not dependent on anything else.

We sometimes offer it as a bland response when someone asks, "How are you?" "Good. And you?"—even though our inner lives might be crumbling.

We use it to commend an obedient pet ("Good dog"). We half-heartedly congratulate someone we actually envy ("Good for you"). *Good* can mean many things. So what do we mean when we say that God is good?

If I can be a bit technical to start, God's goodness means that he has both the ability and the intention to work for the welfare of his people and his creation—for their benefit. His goodness means that he always does what is right. There is no evil, no ill will, no injustice in him.

God does not need to consult a manual to be good. He does not look to some standard apart from himself—he is the standard of goodness. Therefore, good is anything that reflects his character. Evil is anything that opposes his character and will. The way God acts and what he values determine what is good.

Let me give you an example. In the creation account of Genesis 1, God repeatedly declared the goodness of creation. He spoke the world into being and then made the judgment that it is good by simply observing its goodness. His opinion on creation defines the standard. *Life is good. Creation and order are good.* After making his image bearers, he saw that his entire creation was very good. Genesis 2 zooms in on the creation of Adam and Eve, and we learn that Eve's formation was the response to a "not good" situation. God said it was not good that Adam was alone. So God, in his goodness, created a helper. Intimate relationship and community are good things because God says so.

In the situation of Shadrach, Meshach, and Abednego, God's goodness has to do with his *ability* and his *willingness* to deliver even in the most difficult circumstances. We can nuance this further. What we learn from this episode is that God's goodness does not mean he will always deliver in the way we want. God's goodness doesn't mean he is always predictable or obedient to our will.

C. S. Lewis captured this important distinction in a short interchange between the Pevensie children and the beavers in *The Lion, the Witch and the Wardrobe*.[2] The children are excited to meet Aslan, the king of Narnia, until they find out he's a lion.

LUCY: Is—is he a man?

MR. BEAVER: Aslan a man! Certainly not. I tell you he is the King of the wood and the son of the great Emperor-beyond-the-Sea. Don't you know who is the King of Beasts? Aslan is a lion—*the* Lion, the great Lion.

SUSAN: Ooh! I'd thought he was a man. Is he—quite safe? I shall feel rather nervous about meeting a lion.

MRS. BEAVER: That you will, dearie, and no mistake. If there's anyone who can appear before Aslan without their knees knocking, they're either braver than most or else just silly.

LUCY: Then he isn't safe?

MR. BEAVER: Safe? Don't you hear what Mrs. Beaver tells you? Who said anything about safe? 'Course he isn't safe. But he's good. He's the King, I tell you.

Safe does not equal good. Safe is predictable and domesticated. God's goodness promises us that *even if* the outcome (or the situation itself) is not what we might have expected, God works for, defends, and always takes care of those who are his. As Neal Plantinga put it, "Besides reliability, 'God's other name is surprise.' "[3] Sometimes God, in his goodness, will do not what we expect but rather what we could never have dreamed.

Thus, cancer does not invalidate God's goodness. Betrayal does not mean that God has forsaken you. In a strange bit of paradox, life's tragedies and God's goodness are not mutually exclusive. While God's goodness does not spare us from life punching us, it does assure us that God is not the one wearing the brass knuckles.

He may not be predictable, but he is good. *Remembering God's goodness builds confidence in God's goodness no matter what is to come.*

REMEMBERING TO WONDER

When I was a college student, I used to get my hair cut by a Vietnamese immigrant named Vin. I loved the way he could fade my hair with the masterstroke of an artist. Second only to his skill in handling a blade was his knack for that all-important social intelligence a barber needs. He wouldn't talk my ear off, but he wouldn't be aloof either.

On one occasion, we were talking about summer plans, and Vin shared his hope to visit Vietnam for the summer. It would be the first time he had visited since he left twenty-five years earlier.

"Wow, that's a long time. How did you end up in the States?" I asked. I was not ready for the story he would share.

As a young adult, Vin fled when the Vietnam War escalated. After packing what he could into a small bag, he joined a desperate, ragtag caravan to make his escape. Using stripped parts from their homes and blue plastic barrels for floats, the group hastily assembled a makeshift raft and set out into the South China Sea. There were more passengers aboard than even a real boat of similar size could safely hold.

The sea tossed them here and there. The harsh winds paused only long enough for the sun to take its turn to bake their resolve and exacerbate their thirst. After only a few days, the raft began to disintegrate in the open ocean. The waves picked apart the raft as if the sea knew how it was held together. Eventually it crumbled into a loose confederation of semi-floating parts. Vin and a few others desperately clung to a piece of plastic tubing while many members of the ragged crew succumbed to dehydration, sharks, and heat.

After about a week, the survivors were spotted and rescued by an Italian cargo ship. Less than a third of the original crew survived. The ship transported Vin to Italy, where he was granted asylum and then learned to cut hair.

Through a series of equally miraculous events, Vin ended up marrying and immigrating to the United States. Over the years, Vin and his wife had children, and he established a profitable barbershop. His is the archetypal story of the American dream, one that I can appreciate and relate to—minus the life-endangering peril.

As Vin and I continued our discussion of his summer plans, barber chairs around us filled and emptied. The bells hanging from the door clanged countless times, heralding the arrival or departure of another customer, while I just sat there in stunned silence and deep thought. God's goodness had so obviously left a fingerprint on every part of Vin's life. *Spared from war? Rescued at sea? Settled in Italy, then in a little suburb outside Washington, DC? Come on. You can't make this stuff up.*

I started rapid-firing questions at him. "What do you think all this means? Why would God have protected you? What greater purpose do you think is in it all?"

"I haven't really thought about it," he casually remarked. That was the end of it. We both felt the awkward silence. I was more stunned by his response than his story. He seemed to feel no sense of awe at the fact that here he was, miles and years from being adrift in an ocean, standing in his own barbershop cutting my hair.

Maybe he was being guarded and withholding his true feelings. Maybe he had already processed it all, or maybe it was too traumatic to go back to. Perhaps his casual attitude was fitting for the scenery; work isn't often the appropriate place to get sentimental and effusive. I know that he is a grateful man, but his response seemed anticlimactic.

Still, his story made me see something about my own heart. If I were to recount my own life story to someone else, would I treat some of the wondrous, miraculous God-interventions the same way? While I may not have experienced the extremes that he did, how often do I overlook the expressions of God's goodness in my own story? If we stop long enough to consider them, our stories can supply countless remembrances of God's specific, personal, and unique goodness.

Since then, I have learned that remembering is different from recalling. Putting events in a timeline, listing people and places, and other rote acts of telling a story—this is the stuff of recalling. *Remembering* considers the significance of those events, people, and places. If recalling involves thinking about the good meal you and I shared, maybe even posting an Insta story about it, remembering is about considering the joy of the conversation, the gratitude we felt for the work that went into the meal, how it may have deepened our friendship.

I may recall how my life had ups and downs. I have to remember how God was with me along the way. How do you know when you are doing one or the other—recalling or remembering? Like Jesus said about other acts of the heart, you can know it by its fruit (Matthew 7:20). While the fruit of recalling might be acknowledging or verifying what happened, remembering leads us to live differently. It evokes a response.

In one sense, remembrance and awe go together. When we remember—not just recall—the ways in which God has been good to us, it leads us to worship him. It also works the other way around. Just as remembering leads us to awe, so awe can lead us to remember.[4] Slow down enough to take in a fiery sunset or watch a steady and life-giving rain shower, and I hope you experience awe. The awe-inspiring created world beckons us to remember the attributes of the God who spoke it into being. Creation calls us to remember the goodness and glory of God.

Psalm 19:1–4 resounds:

The heavens declare the glory of God,
    and the sky above proclaims his handiwork.
Day to day pours out speech,
    and night to night reveals knowledge.
There is no speech, nor are there words,
    whose voice is not heard.
Their voice goes out through all the earth,
    and their words to the end of the world.

In that way, awe can lead you to remember. Just as God faithfully causes the sun to rise and set each day, he has cared for you, led you, and sustained you over countless days and seasons. When you arise in the morning, remember his mercies anew if only for the reason that you woke up. When you are about to enjoy a good meal, remember the way God gives you your daily bread.

Remember the good and faithful care of God even when you did not acknowledge him. And then take note of what happens in your heart as you remember. You will see that you can never just nostalgically remember God's goodness in your life. His goodness always awakens a response. That's how remembering works. It's why God commands his people over and over again to remember.

I know that remembering is easier said than done, especially in the world we live in. We all swim in the ocean of a media culture, constantly inundated by information. Our attention regularly shifts from one thing to the next, and the sheer volume of updates is eroding our ability to even recall all the events and details, let alone remember and reflect.

Decades ago, Neil Postman called it the "now . . . this" effect.[5] Every media stream and news outlet runs this way. A news story about a local tragedy makes way for a disconnected piece about the weather tomorrow, which gives way to the latest sports highlight, all interrupted by commercials trying to sell you the latest Honda or a certain shampoo.

"Now . . . this" tells us that we've thought long enough about the previous story and it's time to move on to the next bit of attention-grabbing news. We carry "now . . . this" distractions in our pockets (or on our hip belts—I'm not judging you). Our mobile notifications tell us to stop whatever we were doing and pay attention to this next tidbit of information.

Social media streams take it to another level. They are always presenting the next bit of "now . . . this" distraction, be it a pithy quote or a viral meme. Modern media keeps the stream continuous. When you binge a Netflix show, you don't even get the time to digest what has happened in the episode you just watched, because the next one starts in 5 . . . 4 . . . 3 . . .

The result is that it's becoming increasingly difficult to consider the significance of an event before the next one demands our attention. We're left with a faint memory of what happened without the necessary reflection to connect to it personally.

The same can happen with our life events. Instead of a story with meaning and purpose, our lives become a timeline of haphazard events. We can lose sight of the grander narrative, the larger story that we are called to live. In essence, we forget more than we have experienced.

As we lose the ability to remember and reflect, we lose our awe. We become numb. If we are impressed, it's only until we receive the next bit of titillation strong enough to overcome our growing tolerance. And the most tragic consequence is that we sit sedated in a world charged with the awe-inspiring glory of God.[6] The expressions of God's goodness get crowded out among status updates and TikTok videos. We forget what he has done amid all the things that we are doing.

There is an antidote, but it is painfully countercultural and perhaps even counterintuitive now. We have to shut off the noise. You have a choice. You can turn off notifications on your phone. The emails, texts, social media likes, status updates, and more can wait. Even the latest COVID-19–related news will still be there when you get to it. If you are brave enough, you can actually turn off your phone for different periods of time: an hour a day, a day a month, and so on.

The important thing to remember (see what I did there?) is that you are not shutting off those channels because technology is evil. Every *no* can enable a greater *yes*. You are saying no to being inundated with more details than you can recall so you can say yes to remembering the important ways God has been good to you.

This is even truer if you are in the valley or facing the fire. The alternative to remembering is to forget, to be pulled and pushed by the whims not only of the world but also of your imagination. When you forget God's goodness, your imagination begins to work overtime. The fire feels even hotter, the valley that much more desolate. Then complaints begin to rise. The voices of self-condemnation grow louder, accusing you of having done something to deserve such a predicament. Resolve weakens. Confidence wanes. Despair sets in.

The difference between hope and despair is remembering that just as God has been good in the past, so he will continue to be good *even if* the circumstances are not to your liking. Hope finds strength not in what is but in what will be. Remembering God's past goodness becomes the kindling for hoping in God's future kindness.

WHEN YOU HAVE ENOUGH

What if your memory of God's goodness in your own life is foggy? The good news is that God has a larger body of work than just our experiences of him. His goodness and steadfast love are often celebrated together in the pages of the Bible. In the Old Testament, the people of God sang, "He is good, for his steadfast love endures forever" (Psalm 136:1). God's steadfast love reminds us of his faithful commitment to us. Not only is he good to us, but he is also good to us for the long haul.

Think about it. Forever is a long time. That means that no matter how long you might be in the valley, your stay there can't exhaust his goodness and love for you. Valley life, desert dwelling, and fiery furnaces have an expiration date. God's loving-kindness does not.

When you find it difficult to trace God's goodness in your own life, widen the circle, increase the sample size. Shadrach, Meshach, and Abednego's confidence in God's goodness came from remembering that the Lord's steadfast love endures forever, both future forever and past forever. Forever covers both what is to come and all that has come before. God's steadfast love had endured way before them. *Insert mind-blown emoji.*

While they may not have been delivered from Babylon's siege of Jerusalem, Shadrach, Meshach, and Abednego could have remembered how Jerusalem had been delivered from another powerful king a few generations before. If you want to read that fascinating story, look up 2 Kings 18–19.

The Israelites could have remembered even further back to God's deliverance from Egypt. The Exodus was the definitive act of God's covenant-keeping, people-protecting good care. Not only is it recounted in the book of Exodus; this example of God's goodness is also sung about often in Psalms. Psalms 105 and 106 form two parts of a song recounting God's provision and goodness. Psalm 106 is especially powerful because it recounts how God continued to show his goodness in justice and mercy, despite the people's unfaithfulness.

Still today, at the annual remembrance of God's redemptive

work, Jewish families gather and sing about God's goodness as part of the Passover seder. Right after the retelling of the Exodus story, they sing a song called "Dayenu," which means, "It would have been enough for us." In call-and-response format, the people sing "Dayenu, dayenu, dayenu" in response to fourteen different lines. With each line, the song leader declares an act of God's deliverance, and the people respond with "Dayenu"—had God stopped there, it would have been enough.

> If He had merely rescued us from Egypt, but had not punished the Egyptians . . .
> If He had merely punished the Egyptians, but had not destroyed their gods . . .
> If He had merely destroyed their gods, but had not slain their firstborn . . .
> If He had merely slain their firstborn, but had not given us their property . . .
> If He had merely given us their property, but had not split the sea for us . . .
> If He had merely split the sea for us, but had not brought us through on dry ground . . .
> If He had merely brought us through on dry ground, but had not drowned our oppressors . . .
> If He had merely drowned our oppressors, but had not supplied us in the desert for forty years . . .
> If He had merely supplied us in the desert for forty years, but had not fed us with manna . . .
> If He had merely fed us with manna, but had not given us the Sabbath . . .
> If He had merely given us the Sabbath, but had not brought us to Mount Sinai . . .
> If He had merely brought us to Mount Sinai, but had not given us the Torah . . .

If He had merely given us the Torah, but not brought us to
   the land of Israel . . .
If He had merely brought us to the land of Israel, but had
   not built us the Temple . . .
We would have been satisfied.[7]

With great cumulative effect, the song traces God's mighty
works through the generations, recounting episode after episode
of his goodness in delivering and establishing his people. The
dayenu song serves as a powerful liturgy of remembrance, both
stirring gratitude for God's acts and reaffirming hope no matter
what might come.

Remembering God's goodness is the foundation of confidence
for a people who suffered through many furnaces at the hands of
many kings. They remember what God has done for their people
as if he had done it directly for them. He's been good thus far, and
that is enough for them. In fact, he has been so good that, in a
dayenu sense, *even if* God should decide to suspend his blessings
of deliverance in their current situation, what they have experienced of his goodness thus far is enough.

In the New Testament, the apostle Paul explained the purpose
of the Scriptures: "Whatever was written in former days was written for our instruction, that through endurance and through the
encouragement of the Scriptures we might have hope" (Romans
15:4). On a scale larger than our own lives, the Scriptures detail
God's faithfulness to his unfaithful people. God's Word is his way
of helping us remember who he is and what he did way before we
breathed our first breath.

In this way, the Scriptures keep us from limiting God's goodness to what we have seen or experienced. They remind us that
his goodness goes beyond our own desires, beyond the extent of
what we believe might directly benefit us. We're sometimes
tempted to relate to God in a quid pro quo manner: "God, I've

done this for you, so now I expect you'll return the favor." But that is not God; that is a genie who does our will.

We will be sorely disappointed when the "not safe but good" God does something different from what we want. When, instead of keeping us out of the fire, God chooses to show himself to us in it, we can miss the goodness of his presence.

So we have to go back to the Scriptures to remember who God is and what he has done. To remember this way is what it means to meditate on the Scriptures. As J. I. Packer described it, "Meditation is the activity of calling to mind, and thinking over, and dwelling on, and applying to oneself, the various things that one knows about the works and ways and purposes and promises of God."[8]

Christian meditation isn't about emptying our minds. Rather, we bring to mind all that God has done for us and has been to us by remembering how he acted in the Scriptures: the promises he made and his faithfulness not to let those promises go unfulfilled. In this, we come to cherish the Scriptures not just as theological principles or ancient Near Eastern history but as our story. The God of the Bible is the God that we worship and look to. He has not changed, no matter how our circumstances may have.

THE NEARNESS OF GOODNESS

Remembering God's goodness isn't just a monastic exercise to be practiced in silence and solitude, though that is a powerful place to do it. I had to learn how to remember during my initiation into the community of the grieving. When the man who taught me to swim passed away, the resulting sorrow and pain threatened to drown me. My hero, the best man in my wedding, was given that unenviable citizenship in Cancerland, and it felt like my whole world was crashing down.

He died slowly over the course of the summer of 2017. He was admitted to the hospital for a routine procedure but never left because his lungs failed. In the all-too-familiar, gut-punching irony of life, while we were worried about his intestinal cancer, it was another part of his body that killed him.

During the two months leading to his passing, I experienced constant wrestling matches between fear and hope in the arena of my heart. One or the other would win, only for a rematch to be declared the next hour. Some days it looked like he would be released, and then the next hour he would be sentenced to more time in the ICU.

What sustained me through the ebb and flow, the starts and stops of promising improvements and turns for the worse, was remembering God's goodness. I had to remember who God is in the face of the daunting fire. But where do you look for God's goodness when your dad is intubated and the days turn into weeks, then months? When the outcome is not what you hoped for?

I had to look beyond my present circumstances, back to the past, in order to gain confidence for the present and future. I spent drives to and from the hospital remembering God's goodness to me and my family over the years. I made a playlist of worship anthems that declared God's ever-present comfort and help.

I remembered how, in his goodness, God planted an immigrant dream in my parents and transplanted them to the United States. He guided them and provided for them when they left behind their families to settle in a country where they didn't even know the language, enduring the racism of being treated as perpetual foreigners. They worked long hours and all sorts of dirty jobs. And through it all, God preserved them.

God sustained our family through seasons when we thought our parents would be torn apart by financial losses, marital difficulties, and betrayals. We certainly did not triumph in every circumstance, nor did we avoid our share of scars and dysfunction.

Yet my sister and I remarked that as much as my parents had nearly messed up our family through a variety of mistakes and mishaps, God's goodness had prevailed.

And if God had been so good thus far, so many times in spite of us, how could we doubt him now? His goodness did not spare us, but it sustained us. God's goodness doesn't necessarily preclude tears. But his body of work is enough to trust him. In the moments before Dad breathed his last, my family stood around his hospital bed, partaking in bread and cup, the sacramental reminder of just how good God is. We meditated on the way Jesus sought out lonely sinners, how he grieved with the mourning, how God had so much compassion for his suffering people. Choking back sobs, we sung tear-soaked hymns of old, songs that declared the story of his goodness to the world.

Even today, as I continue to walk the journey of grief—learning to endure the unpredictable waves of sorrow and to care for a widow at the same time—I trust God's goodness to sustain me in whatever might come. I am confident in him even though I do not know how this will turn out. God may not be predictable, but he is good.

How have you experienced God's sustaining goodness? At the time, you may not have even perceived it as God's goodness toward you. But as you look back, I hope you can see God's cumulative, sustaining dayenu song in your life. Maybe in the form of endurance or comfort. Provision or protection. A timely word, a hope-kindling promise, the sitting-in-the-ashes presence of a loyal friend.

Can I encourage you to look even a little further back? No matter what the constellation of dayenu moments in your life may look like, if you are a believer in Christ, you have the same North Star as I do. While we each have a dayenu song composed of unique verses, we all share a common foundational verse.

If you had merely promised redemption and restoration . . .
dayenu.
If you had merely come in flesh to walk among us . . . da-
yenu.
If you had merely been tempted in every way and not
sinned . . . dayenu.
If you had merely sympathized with our weaknesses . . . da-
yenu.
If you had merely healed the sick . . . dayenu.
If you had merely taught about the kingdom of God . . . da-
yenu.
If you had merely made the sacrifice for sins . . . dayenu.
If you had merely forgiven us . . . dayenu.
If you had merely overcome death by rising from the
grave . . . dayenu.
If you had merely adopted us as sons and daughters . . . da-
yenu.

At each step of the unfolding drama of the gospel story, God
showed his goodness to a lost, rebellious, broken humanity. Then
he demonstrated the fullness of his love, the culmination of his
goodness, at the Cross—forgiving sinners and punishing sin.

The first part of the *even if* declaration is anchored in this objective reality: God demonstrated his goodness and steadfast love
by saving us from the death that sin demanded. That means that
no matter what happens to me, my identity and my security are
found in the unchangeable and satisfactory work of Christ on the
cross!

On the night Jesus was betrayed, he called his disciples to remember (Luke 22:19). When we partake of the bread and cup,
we remember the goodness of God both past and future—
gratitude and hope come together at that meal.

We look back in gratitude at the great sacrifice of the Son of God on our behalf—the Son of Man who was betrayed and gave his life as a ransom for us. God paid the ultimate price for my ultimate good. We remember God's goodness in his past deliverance.

We also look forward in hope to his return, to the day when we will no longer have to partake of this meal as a way of remembering, because we will eat with him face to face. That means that no matter what we might be facing today, we know that it will ultimately end with an invitation to eat with God at his table. We remember God's goodness in what is to come.

Let those remembrances form the hope that he can deliver you from whatever you are facing now. *Even if* that deliverance should take longer or come in different ways than you might expect, God is good and he will continue to be good to you.

3

More Than a New Year's Resolution

"I can't do this. I give up," my son Benjamin declared in frustration, throwing his unfolded laundry back into the pile. My beloved third son is fire and ice, all in or all out. When something captivates him, good luck trying to pry him away. He can sit for hours with his Legos, building, destroying, then rebuilding a never-ending variety of scenarios where the villains meet their demise.

When he gives up on something, it might as well not even exist. If he can't figure out a piece of something, he will completely bail. Sitting there in front of a mound of laundry, he was throwing in the white flag of his Kung Fu Panda underwear.

As he sprang up to go play with his Legos, my wife's words froze him midrise, locking him in a yoga-like squat pose: "Do not go anywhere. Try again. Don't give up so easily."

After a bit of warring back and forth, he wilted back down to the ground, grudgingly obeying her. In our household, we say that begrudging obedience is obedience nonetheless—a principle that has literally saved the life of each of our five kids at many points in their individual portfolios of rebellion.

"What you're lacking isn't the skill, Ben. It's the resolve to learn it. Try again until you get it right." With the patience of a highly paid instructor, my bride showed him how to fold his own laundry, painstakingly detailing each step. Our lives have never been the same.

Over the sitcom that is our parenting journey, we have had to teach our children the resolve to make other domestic contributions: taking out the trash, doing the dishes, vacuuming, cleaning their rooms, and so on. Sometimes, like when learning to fold the laundry, they needed the resolve to stick with an unfamiliar task in order to learn how to do it correctly. Most of the time, they needed the resolve to do a task they simply did not feel like doing in the moment. Resolve is a necessary life skill.

Resolve is also an important part of faith. It is the strength of will that flows from deep belief. Sometimes it can be seen in a refusal to compromise our convictions, those deeply held beliefs about how we should live and how we should treat others. In other places, resolve can look like endurance, the resilient strength that allows us not to drown even when the water is over our heads.

While it is generally seen as a noble attribute, resolve is only as admirable as the beliefs that supply it. People who believe that the world is out to get them will be labeled paranoid. Those who refuse to take safety precautions because they believe in their own invincibility will be seen as naive and reckless. Depending on the belief sustaining it, resolve can be either stubbornness or against-all-odds stick-with-it-ness.

The *even if* life is marked by resolve that flows from the deep belief in God's goodness.

In the last chapter, I tried to define and nuance what God's goodness means with the hope that you will spend the rest of your life exploring and enjoying his goodness more deeply. The first part of the *even if* declaration is confidence in God's goodness, and the second is the resolve to worship our good God—all while life might not be going the way we imagined. Without the belief in God's goodness, there can be no lasting resolve to worship him.

The two parts of the *even if* declaration go hand in hand. If you doubt God's goodness, you can begin to believe that you are abandoned, facing the fire alone, left to your own resources to save yourself. Without resolve, you might fold in the face of the fire or go to the opposite extreme of avoiding the pain altogether. With a kind of myopic optimism, you might refuse to acknowledge furnaces for what they are—hot, uncomfortable, and deadly.

In Daniel 3, while Shadrach, Meshach, and Abednego had confidence that God could save them, they left open the real possibility that he might not. They believed in a God whose goodness extended well beyond their own experience of him. They did not know how the story was going to unfold. Yet with firm resolve, these three young men declared their intention to worship him regardless of how it turned out for them. Here is an even simpler way to put the *even if* declaration:

Our God can save us (*belief in God's goodness*),

but *even if* he doesn't, we won't worship any other God (*resolve*).

This chapter is about unpacking what *even if* resolve looks like. As we have already seen, resolve can take many forms: stubbornness, fortitude, endurance, and conviction are just a few that come to mind.

This is just as true when it comes to what faith-driven resolve looks like. In fact, many sincere believers think (and will be glad to tell you) that such resolve is simply the strength of your will to get through whatever you are facing. What arises from this understanding is a whole host of apocryphal-like sayings:

"God helps those who help themselves."

"God will never give you more than you can handle."

"God's going to use this for some greater good."

"Think of all the people you will be able to help as a result of this."

In her cancer memoir, *Everything Happens for a Reason*, Duke professor Kate Bowler described these chilling responses.[1] During her treatment for stage 4 cancer, she decided to chronicle the journey and send it in to the *New York Times* as an op-ed. What resulted was a litany of comments and testimonies attempting to strengthen her resolve, many quite unsuccessfully.

Some people tried to minimize her struggle by reminding her of what she had: "At least you have a son" or "At least you were able to get treatment." Her suffering was being weighed on a balance scale, where as long as her situation was better than someone else's, she had a foundation for resolve. She could endure it, the logic went, because she had so many advantages that the letter writer did not.

Others attempted to strengthen her by telling her to suck it up and press forward. It wasn't as bad as she made it out to be. An army of Tony Robbins-type impersonators gave her pep talks telling her that because the letter writer had overcome something similar or even far worse (in the writer's own eyes), she could endure.

Still other responses sought to leverage her vulnerability into a teaching moment. These "prophets" pointed out the lesson that God surely had in mind for her. And because of the value of this lesson, she could endure and get through the painful treatment process. Even if she didn't survive, there would be a lesson in her death that would be taught to others.

While they might have arisen from sincere intentions and seemed compassionate in the moment (at least in the letter writer's head), all of these responses appeared tone deaf at best in their attempts to strengthen resolve.

A telltale sign of attempts to form such "pseudo-resolve" is the comparisons from which they derive. The strength of the advice or encouragement will come from comparing our situation with others (most often their own). We'll hear anecdotes of how someone encountered a similar or more difficult situation and came out on top. (You rarely hear the ones who didn't survive.) We then talk ourselves into thinking that because we have it so much better than others, we should be able to endure. Pseudo-resolve gets delivered in a pep talk.

But the resolve that flows from such comparisons is frail because the objects of comparison are always shifting. Our situations and the situations of those we compare ourselves with are in flux. On top of that, comparisons are subjective and, like beauty, are in the eye of the beholder for better or worse.

When these motivational clichés and approaches do not result in the intended resolve, oftentimes the advice givers move on from us, as if we are hopeless cases with not enough faith. Christians are, after all, notorious for shooting our wounded.

I believe there is a better way. The only lasting foundation for a persevering and faith-filled resolve will come from the unchanging, incomparable nature of who God is. When God's character provides perspective and strength from outside our own situations, resolve becomes firm. That kind of resolve rests not on our willpower, nor even necessarily on our understanding of the situation, but on our confidence in God's goodness.

RECOGNIZE A COUNTERFEIT

After graduating from college, I lived for about two years in Asia, and before I knew any better, one of my favorite things to do there was to shop for knockoffs. While I don't really care about high-end designer goods, I relished the challenge of finding a hard-to-distinguish copycat at an alarmingly low price. I may have even given a bag or three as gifts to family when I returned from my travels.

I also loved finding the really bad versions: a "Guci" bag (misspelled exactly like that), a "Nice Air" swoosh T-shirt made by someone whose grasp of English phonics was clearly lacking. During those years, I always had a passable pair of "Fay-Ban" aviators in my bag and a "Faux-lex" watch on my wrist.

The thing about counterfeits is that they never last as long as the real thing. I was aware of that when browsing, so I haggled down the price as if I had a master's degree in trade negotiations. The knockoff Barcelona jersey will last maybe a few months or a few washes before the lettering peels. The watch will stop working. The stitching will come apart. The thing is, no one complains about the quality of a knockoff, because you get what you pay for. You almost expect it not to last. When it breaks, you just get another one—no problem.

I've since come to recognize why purchasing counterfeit goods is wrong: the way it promotes brand elitism, infringes patents and copyrights, and feeds unhealthy consumerism. The money from counterfeit goods can also fund other illegal activities. A seemingly harmless shopping hobby can have harmful consequences.

The consequences are far more serious for the important things in life. No one wants knockoff virtue. Counterfeit love destroys a heart, hardening it and locking it off from true intimacy. Knockoff kindness limits relationships to the exchange of pleasantries, keeping relationships shallow. Fake loyalty leads to the worst kinds of betrayal. Even resolve can be counterfeited.

Such counterfeit resolve sometimes masquerades as overconfident faith, the telltale refusal to accept the possibility that God might not do what you want. Statements like "I just know God is going to . . ." or "God's not going to let . . ." reveal a bold certainty that God will not do otherwise. Such faith can sound overly triumphal and out of touch—a kind of counterfeit hope.

I had the honor of grieving with a friend as she was walking with her husband through the valley of the shadow of death. From his diagnosis to his departure, the journey lasted an excruciatingly short two months. My friend was amazingly resolute in her belief. She would quote Bible verses and assure us that her faith was strong because she just knew that God could and would heal him. She refused to see any other possibility.

At first glance, it looked like steady, faith-filled resolve in the face of a menacing foe. But her resolve was built on the belief that God would do exactly as she believed he could. She hadn't yet formed the resolve to worship God no matter how it turned out. So convinced that God would keep them from the fire, she was missing the very real opportunity to experience him in the furnace. God wanted to meet her in her fear, anger, disappointment, and sorrow. She wanted to meet him only in the triumph of a miraculous healing.

I realize that there is a tension here. We want to continue to believe that God can heal, but we also want to prepare for the possibility that he may not. How can anyone faithfully live in that tension without becoming cynical or out of touch?

In the two weeks before her husband passed, something shifted in my friend's faith. She didn't stop quoting Scripture or listening to inspiring music. She continued to encourage people— but with a sobriety that was previously missing. There were lots more tears intermixed with her usual tender and soft words. A sense of loss accompanied times of gratitude.

Most onlookers would say she finally accepted the reality that her husband was going to die, but I think something deeper was occurring. It was not just the reality of her husband's death awakening her but also the reality that the God whom they had served together for so many years was with her and worthy of worship *even if* her husband died. She resolved to worship God even in the ashes, even with her tears. She resolved to endure every up and down because she believed that God would give her every-thing she needed. Triumphant optimism transposed into genuine resolve.

How can you tell triumphant optimism from genuine resolve? Especially when counterfeit resolve seems so hopeful and confi-dent? Any inspector will tell you that the best way to distinguish between a knockoff and the real thing is to study the original. Take the time to really understand the characteristics of the au-thentic thing, and you will be able to spot a pretender.

Even if–type resolve begins by acknowledging the real trouble, doubts, and fears you are facing. We admit our uncertainty about how things will turn out without bowing down to the despair that wants to be its wingman. Let me state the obvious: resolve to wor-ship God comes precisely at the moment when our confidence in God's goodness might shake.

You don't resolve to do something without a challenge or threat. Conviction and endurance are virtues that we develop when life tries to bully us into giving up or compromising. When your confidence in God's goodness is challenged by the real heat and flames of the furnace in front of you, you have three choices:

- Let the situation intimidate you into losing confidence in God.
- Ignore or minimize the difficulty of the situation.
- Call the situation what it is, and resolve to trust in the God who's been good to you thus far.

In this way, genuine resolve has an "in-touchness" to it, believ-ing the promises of God with a measure of grit and sobriety. Just as genuine, biblical faith lives with one foot in the realities of life in this broken world and with the other in the resurrection-shaped realities of God's present and coming kingdom, so the re-solve that flows from it will be both earthly and celestial.

When we resolve, we choose to live out of our confidence in

God's goodness. We resolve to worship God *even if* the hard situation itself doesn't resolve or doesn't turn out the way we want. And in doing so, we bring our fears and disappointment, choosing to trust the God who loves us and will be good to us.

Resolve in the *even if* sense involves surrender—not to be confused with its own unique counterfeit: resignation. Resignation is the passive and fatalistic "whatever happens, happens" attitude that refuses to take responsibility. Its motto is "Everything happens for a reason." Surrender is the trust-filled response that says, "No matter what happens, I trust the God who is for me." Surrender is an active choice, the laying down of your plans, your opposition, even your desires.

Resignation is more like rolling over, hoping that the will of the Fates doesn't kick you too hard in the side. Because it is passive, you don't need to recommit to resignation like you do with surrender. Oftentimes you will have to surrender again and again, each time resolving to trust the goodness of God. Surrender involves dying to the desire to be in control. And as you surrender with each new challenge, you will come to experience the power of genuine resolve: it comes not from the strength of your will but rather from surrender to his.

BE THE BEST PREACHER YOU KNOW

The sons of Korah showed us the beauty of resolve in the midst of the complexity of life. In Psalm 42, they declared their intense longing for God, like a deer panting for flowing streams (verse 1). God felt distant. Tears abounded. Nostalgically they remembered when God was celebrated with a parade befitting a championship sports team. Joy. Praise. A festal shout even.

But the memory served as a painful dirge of a time gone by, the reminder of what they had lost. It might have been like that then, but it wasn't that way anymore. This longing for God is the kind you experience during a memorial service or wake, not in the buildup to a birth.

Then resolve shows up:

Why are you cast down, O my soul,
    and why are you in turmoil within me?
Hope in God; for I shall again praise him,
    my salvation and my God. (verses 5–6)

Faced with the reality of loss, the sons resolved to hope in the God who saves. They literally spoke to their souls.

In the second half of the song, they wrestled with the feeling of being forgotten by God, amplified by the taunts of an enemy who continued to oppress them. In all-too-relatable tones, the psalm asks why: "Why have you forgotten me?" "Why do I go mourning?" (verse 9). They called their situation what it was.

In crescendo-like fashion, the sons repeated the refrain and reminded us of their resolve:

Why are you cast down, O my soul,
    and why are you in turmoil within me?
Hope in God; for I shall again praise him,
    my salvation and my God. (verse 11)

Resolve even refashioned the complaint.

In Psalm 43, the sons confidently asserted their hope. God would vindicate. He would restore. He would defend. Their longing shifted from what was to what could be. They longed for a particular future, one that they knew God could bring about because he was their salvation and God. Calling a situation what it is and trusting God no matter how it goes doesn't preclude us from telling him our desires. In fact, surrendering our desires requires us to name them.

Even with such assertions, resolve was required. They commanded their souls again to hope in the One who could bring about the future they longed for:

> Why are you cast down, O my soul,
>   and why are you in turmoil within me?
> Hope in God; for I shall again praise him,
>   my salvation and my God. (verse 5)

The same resolve holds together the grief for what was, the anguish over what is, and the longing for what could be.

In this way, the two psalms show us a robust picture of *even if* resolve. "*Even if* I never get back to that place I was, even if my enemies oppress me now, even if the future I long for should not come about, I put my hope in the God who has been, is, and will be my salvation." Literally talking to their own souls, they reminded themselves to hope in God.

David Martyn Lloyd-Jones had a helpful way of saying this: "Most of your unhappiness in life is due to the fact that you are listening to yourself instead of talking to yourself."[2] Even though he was talking about spiritual depression, I think his diagnosis is also applicable to growing our resolve. Instead of listening to ourselves, we need to preach to ourselves: "Why are you cast down, O my soul? Hope in God . . ." Easier said than done.

We all have an inner monologue by which we interpret the world around us. We interpret events that happen to us, words spoken to us, even nonverbal expressions. Our monologues are usually fashioned around a recurring narrative, the stories we tell ourselves about who we are. All throughout the day, the voices in our heads give a color commentary on why so-and-so did such-and-such and what we must do in response.

These inner voices amplify and minimize. They amplify self-doubt and self-condemnation, and they minimize the truthfulness of any feedback saying we might be at fault. They declare us to be failures and unworthy of love and at the same time explain why someone else is to blame. And they are always believable because, well, they sound like us. In fact, we accept their interpretations and verdicts so unquestioningly that I could probably stop saying "They tell us . . ." and just say "We tell ourselves . . ."

What Martyn Lloyd-Jones suggested and the sons of Korah demonstrated is that, instead of listening to the podcasts of our own voices, we must subscribe to the truth of God's Word. We must learn to preach over the voices we are accustomed to heeding.

You have the opportunity to build a library of little in-the-moment sermons reminding yourself of God's goodness and nearness. No one else needs to know. You don't have to become famous. You don't even need to preach your sermons aloud, although I wouldn't be surprised if they come out in bits of encouragement you give to others. With enough repetition, you can become—and, I would insist, you have to become—the best preacher you know.

Preach to yourself as a way of remembering what is true, even in the face of what seems to be the contrary. Preach to yourself in order to believe the things that are true no matter how you might feel about them, no matter what your own voices say. Resolve will grow in the soil of the mini sermons you preach to yourself.

As I encourage you in this, I anticipate that you will face the same dilemma that every aspiring preacher does: how to find good material. You don't have to look far. By reflecting on God's goodness a little more closely, you'll have all the content you need.

What Have You Done for Me Lately?

As we saw in the last chapter, God's goodness goes beyond your own experience of it, beyond what God has done personally for you. That means there is a much bigger body of work you can draw from.

A fancy way to say this is that God's goodness has both an objective and a subjective weight to it. *Objective* refers to the quality of something in and of itself. *Subjective* refers to your own opinion, often based on the benefit you feel from something. An objective critique of your fashion sense might be based on the latest trends and the cost of putting your wardrobe together. A subjective critique is based on the colors you like and the deeply held belief that clip-on bowties should be avoided if you are over the age of ten.

Our consumer-driven society places the subjective above the objective in many cases. Much of our sense of loyalty to anyone or anything is determined by whether our needs are being met. "How will this relationship benefit my situation? What's in it for me?" In a consumer relationship, my subjective needs are of the utmost importance, or the relationship will be terminated.

We can even relate to God primarily on the subjective level, even on the consumer level, as if he were a divine provider of spiritual services. In this kind of relationship, I will define God's goodness based on the subjective, meaning how I've experienced his goodness in my life: the blessings (as I define them) that God has given me or the way that he makes me feel.

In the eighteenth century, the pastor-scholar Jonathan Edwards described the dynamic of enjoying God in both an objective and a subjective sense.[3] He explained that one of the truest signs of a work of God is a desire for God based on who he is, with little to no immediate thought for self-benefit or self-interest (subjective). The objective enjoyment of God comes when we recognize the inherent goodness of God whether or not we feel as if we have experienced it.

Objective enjoyment and subjective enjoyment of God don't have to be mutually exclusive. They actually go hand in hand and even lead to each other. We rejoice in God because of the objective excellence of his character. He embodies beauty. There is nothing and no one more pure, faithful, awesome, or wise than he. He is just, and everything he does, he does out of the perfection of his own character. He has no beginning and no end. He is so patient. He can't do wrong. He is good! That doesn't depend on what my life looks like. It's who he is. Objective.

Yet those perfections and excellencies have subjective benefit to me: He shows me mercy. He is dependable because he will not abandon me. His sovereign plans are his to reveal. He alone has the ability to change my heart. His faithfulness has sustained me through countless dayenu moments. His forgiveness enables me to forgive others. In this sense, the objective grounds the subjective, and the subjective gives expression to the objective.

We could sum it up this way:

Subjective: I worship you for *what* you have done for me.
Objective: I enjoy you for *who* you are.

When you imagine God's goodness, what comes to mind? Is it primarily subjective or objective? If your answer is "Subjective," you aren't alone. I think most of us fashion our relationships with God around subjective enjoyment. Listen to most people's testimonies, and they will tell about the way God delivered them or cared for them personally. This is not a bad thing. Our personal God is at work in our lives in a thousand ways.

The confidence and resolve that form the *even if* declaration come from living in the rhythm of the objective and subjective enjoyment of God's goodness. We need the objective because his goodness will not always fit our expectations or our desires. In those times, the resolve to worship him will come from our objective enjoyment—he deserves worship because of who he is regardless of what we might be experiencing.

Shadrach, Meshach, and Abednego resolved to worship God out of the conviction that he was worthy of their worship *even if* he didn't do what they wanted. Even though God had let their city be captured, they resolved to stand on the objective truth that he is good, even if their subjective experience meant that they were going to die in the fire. There was no doubt in their minds who alone was deserving of their worship. Resolve flowed from confidence in God's objective worthiness.

We can all grow in objectively enjoying God by study. Thankfully, there are men and women who have gone before us, seeking to understand and describe who God is. You might want to start with a study on the names of God throughout the Bible or maybe a deeper dive into a systematic theology that categorizes his attributes. Growing in the objective enjoyment of God is more than just an intellectual pursuit. Think of it as a way to grow in your confidence in God's goodness.

C. S. Lewis explained it this way: "We are taught . . . to 'give thanks to God for His great glory,' as if we owed Him more thanks for being what He necessarily is than for any particular benefit He confers upon us; and so indeed we do and to know God is to know this."[4]

Standing at a Crossroads

Let me offer one final picture of how the objective and subjective enjoyment of God strengthens resolve. The good news of how God came to save us has both an objective and a subjective element to it. The writer of Hebrews points to the example of Jesus's resolve as a way to encourage us: "Let us run with endurance the race that is set before us, looking to Jesus, the founder and perfecter of our faith, who for the joy that was set before him endured the cross, despising the shame, and is seated at the right hand of the throne of God" (12:1–2).

Jesus resolved to endure the Cross, trusting in the joy that was before him. He endured the shame and brutality of crucifixion. There was little subjective enjoyment in it for him. Yet his confidence in the wisdom, justice, and faithfulness of God gave him the resolve to endure it. He fixed his eyes on the joy promised to him. It didn't make the pain of the Cross any less, but it was enough to help him endure. The objective goodness of God strengthened his resolve even as the subjective benefit would come only after his gruesome sacrificial death.

And Jesus's resolve gives us the endurance to run our race. Just as Jesus resolved to obey the Father's will because of his confidence in God's good plan, so we are called to run our races with similar confidence. We can have confidence in God's goodness because, through the Cross, God has done eternal good to us.

He has demonstrated his objective perfection: justice, holiness, mercy, love, and wisdom in punishing sin. And we have received the subjective benefits: forgiveness, adoption, reconciliation, and atonement. Confidence in the objective and subjective goodness of God comes from the intersection of those two beams of wood. We can enjoy both in the gospel story. What kind of God is so wise as to punish sin and forgive sinners in the same act? What kind of God humbles himself to pay the price for rebels?

Our God is just and merciful, powerful and humble, full of wrath over sin and overflowing in grace toward sinners—no one is objectively like him. And our lives bear the fruit of a thousand subjective blessings flowing from what he did for us at the Cross. He is for us. Nothing separates us from his love. He calls us sons and daughters. All this is ours because of Jesus's resolve to do what the Father called him to do.

In fact, Jesus's resolve strengthens our resolve to declare our *even if* as we carry our own crosses, as we endure our own unique sets of sufferings. I see it in my own story as well as the stories of friends around me.

I knew a gifted worship leader whose love of leading God's people in song was second only to her devotion to her husband and two daughters. Several years into her marriage, she started getting sick frequently. What started as body aches ended up debilitating her, forcing her to be bedridden for days on end. The sickness eventually overtook her entire body. Finally her lungs began to fail. As we prayed for her, her husband sent out a letter to share about a difficult decision they had to make. It was his own *even if* declaration:

Today was a long day. This week has been a long day. This year has been one long day. . . . There is nothing that humanity can do to save [my wife], it is out of their hands. . . . Now it is in God's hands. . . . Barring a miracle, she will be glorifying God in His very presence by this Thursday. Why Thursday? Well, that date was chosen because it is her birthday, and there is nothing that could be a better gift for her at this stage than to give her the chance to see God for the first time on her birthday.

I know what some people are thinking, how can I treat such a morbid and devastating event so lightly? Well, it's because I believe. I believe that Christ incarnated himself, died on the cross, and rose from the dead to redeem his people. In short, it's because both [my wife] and myself believe the radically powerful Bible verse that popped up on my phone today: "To die is gain."

. . . No matter what happens, I will love God with all of my heart, mind and soul. Whether she is healed from her lung disease so that she can die later, or whether she dies tomorrow, I will worship God. Why? Because no matter what, God will still be God, which means his righteousness and holiness and love and grace and sovereignty will still be worthy of my all-out adoration. Which God do you worship?

She ended up going to her heavenly home that week. It was a peaceful but bittersweet goodbye as resolve was tested with sadness and loss. Trust in God's goodness was superimposed onto the reality of a broken world. They celebrated her life and worshipped God in the midst of the ashes.

Jesus's resolve makes yours possible. God's goodness demonstrated ultimately on the cross gives you courage to look soberly into whatever furnace you are facing and to resolve to worship him *even if* . . . Sometimes your resolve will be a bold shout of defiance against an intimidating foe. Sometimes it will be the faintest of whispers as you are barely holding on. Whether in strength or weakness, your *even if* counts because, through it all, Jesus promises he will never leave you nor forsake you (Hebrews 13:5). He is the God we trust and worship.

PART 2

ENCOUNTERING OUR *COUNTER IFS*

London's underground rail system sprawls beneath the city, connecting its various boroughs like a vascular system. Much like any other metropolitan subway, a tube train arrives at the station, passengers offload, then new ones get on. The London Underground is known especially for its iconic slogan Mind the Gap. Maybe you've seen it on T-shirts or memes.

Because many of its stations feature sharply curved platforms, a space inevitably forms between the doorway of the train car and the station platform. The slogan is stamped on the platform edge every few feet, warning passengers of the potentially treacherous space between where they are standing and the train they are trying to board. One station on the Northern Line even broadcasts the warning over the station speakers, a cantankerous voice from the 1970s bellowing, "Mind the gap!"

It's a fitting illustration of the challenges of living an *even if* life. As we attempt to grow in our confidence in God's goodness and our resolve to worship him, life will throw many surprises our way. Inevitably we will have to mind the gap between the train car of reality and the platform of our expectations.

We will even have to mind the gaps others create for us by their expectations. The child who lives to earn his parent's approval understands this all too well. Even into adulthood, all it takes to feel the gap is a look of disdain or a passive-aggressive comment. The verdict is clear: "You didn't meet the expectations" or "You didn't meet them like [so-and-so's] kid did." The gnawing feeling of being a disappointment—whether to ourselves or someone else—is what makes the gap such an exhausting place to be.

The good news is that the gap between what we expect and what we actually face is the very space in which the *even if* declaration takes shape. After all, if life always went the way we wanted, we wouldn't need to be reminded of God's goodness, nor would we need to strengthen our resolve to worship him. It's precisely in our attempts to mind the gap that we can either declare *even if* or get stuck in what I'll call *counter if*s—the patterns of thinking and believing that focus on us, not God.

*Counter if*s can be subtle; you may not realize they are directing you. You don't actively and intentionally decide to live by a *counter if*. It becomes more like a way of dealing with life, a patchwork series of responses that over time becomes a quilt. Like pesky weeds in a garden, they creep in and are unnoticeable until they bloom. But that does not mean they are harmless. *Counter if*s can leave you feeling stuck, disappointed, even cynical about your situation.

While there are numerous expressions they can take, *counter if*s fall generally into three patterns: *only if, if only,* and *what if.* We will look at each in turn, considering the ways they hold us back and how God can turn a *counter if* into an *even if.* But first let's look a little more closely at the gap.

4

I Want It My Way

I send off my final email and am excited to get home and relax. The *swoosh* as the email disappears signals the end of the day like the closing bell of the stock market. I quickly review my day. *Meetings went fairly well. The counseling session I led seemed to be helpful. Study time was filled with a few rabbit trails but not more than usual. At least I have the beginnings of a sermon to show for it. I wish I could have that one conversation back, but I did the best I could. Overall, not a bad day.*

Beyond those few highlights and one lowlight, I am too brain dead to think about much else. I conclude, *I've worked so hard today. I deserve a little rest.* If I'm honest with myself, I think I even deserve a little acknowledgment for a hard day's work. I pack up my stuff, set my desk in order, and head home, lingering on the thought of what I deserve as compensation for my labors. With each minute of my commute home, my sense of entitlement expands. My desire for rest and validation fuels visions of "me time" and leisure, fading out any responsibilities awaiting me at home. *It would be nice to get some rest and appreciation* grows into *I* need *rest and appreciation.*

By the time I get to my driveway, the desire-turned-need has become a full-on decree: *I will get the rest and appreciation I deserve. After all,* I reason to myself, *it's a simple expectation—nothing more than a hardworking, sacrificial servant like me deserves.*

At the height of my quasi-delusional fantasy, I actually imagine my kids and wife dropping what they are doing at the sound of the garage door opening, forming a gauntlet, and declaring in adoring unison, "All hail our returning father, who has changed the world today and deserves nothing but the highest praise! Let us give him what he has earned and leave him alone!" As I enter the house, I full-on *demand* what I imagined in the car.

Needless to say, reality always turns out different from my imagination. The tragic part of my rude awakening is that when I don't get what I demand, I mete out a punishment, usually through some combination of irritability, zoning out, and withdrawing to my bedroom. *Fitting consequences, of course, for a family that is so ungrateful for all that I have done for them.*

Did you catch the progression? What started out as a sincere desire for rest became a need, grew into an expectation, and reared its ugly head as a demand that no one was ready to meet.[1] This mutation occurs in so many places in my life, and by God's grace, I've gotten better at recognizing when it takes place in my heart. I have come to see that I don't need even twenty minutes to go from desire to demand to the resultant disappointment and punishment. During the COVID-19 quarantine, I was stunned to see the entire birthing cycle of a demand happen in the seconds it took to go from my makeshift home office to the kitchen after my last virtual meeting of the day.

What happens on my commute and in numerous mini episodes on any given day can also develop in more significant areas over longer seasons of life. Desires can slow cook over years, marinating into expectations that subconsciously rule our lives. A five-year plan can become a will and testament, our blueprint for happiness submitted to God not for his approval but for his rubber-stamping.

The desire to be married turns into expectations of when, to whom, and what the wedding colors will be. The longing for children becomes expectations of when, how many, and what they will be like. The ambition to have a successful career becomes expectations of what we will have achieved by what age. The hope for comfort and security turns into the unspoken expectation that we will have a clean bill of health for our "productive" years. Though we might describe our wants in various ways—desires, hopes, ambitions—the progression is similar.

DON'T BLAME THE GPS

Before we talk more about the results of this progression, let me stress that I'm not coming down on desires. Desires are not bad in themselves. In fact, it's impossible not to have desires. The Scriptures assume we will: "Delight yourself in the LORD, and he will give you the desires of your heart" (Psalm 37:4). Everyone has desires for love, security, purpose, and meaning. We have desires to be happy. Even the desire for rest or affirmation isn't sinful.

One of the ways that God demonstrates his goodness to us is the way in which he satisfies our desires. He fulfills our deepest longings for love and intimacy ultimately in relationship with himself. In his kindness, he also fulfills our longings to be known by giving us the gifts of community and vital friendships. He even meets the deep desires we didn't know we had until they are met in him.

C. S. Lewis described how desires work:

Creatures are not born with desires unless satisfaction for those desires exists. A baby feels hunger: well, there is such a thing as food. A duckling wants to swim: well, there is such a thing as water. Men feel sexual desire: well, there is such a thing as sex. If I find in myself a desire which no experience in this world can satisfy, the most probable explanation is that I was made for another world. If none of my earthly pleasures satisfy it, that does not prove that the universe is a fraud. Probably earthly pleasures were never meant to satisfy it, but only to arouse it, to suggest the real thing.[2]

Lewis's point is that desires are meant to be satisfied. In this way, God uses our desires to draw us to himself. They are meant to act like a GPS pointing us to the destination our hearts ultimately long for, to the God who alone can give us what we really desire. While some desires might be partially fulfilled by the good things God provides us, all those things are meant to whet our appetites and stir our longings for a good God who ultimately satisfies.

So desires are not the problem. It's what we do with our desires—how we attempt to satisfy them—that makes all the difference. The challenge of living in our broken world is that our desires can often be intercepted and misdirected away from God. Instead of following the GPS to the intended destination, we stop at a myriad of waypoints along the route.

We can look to people or material things to fulfill us in ways that they were never intended to. What is meant as an appetizer gets confused for the main meal. God can be for us a sixteen-ounce, dry-aged, bone-in rib eye cooked medium rare, but we gorge ourselves on cheeseballs and lose our appetites. We miss out on the deeper, more lasting satisfaction by settling for temporary, junk food titillations.

Desires can also mislead when they become all consuming,

growing into expectations and then demands that put our needs and preferences above everything and everyone else. Satisfying our desires exactly as we wish becomes paramount, and the result is self-absorption and entitlement. We will then do whatever we can to fulfill our desires, letting them control us in the form of demands. As desires become demands, the fulfillment of those demands becomes the metric by which we judge ourselves, the quality of our lives, and our contentment.

It's not too long before we start to evaluate God this way. We begin to view him not as the source of our satisfaction but as the means to get what we want. We can subtly build the expectation that God, if he loved us, if he were really good, would give us what we ask in precisely the way we expect it.

We don't get that way overnight. These kinds of expectations start out as the sincerest of desires often with a kingdom-minded quality to them. We begin by looking to God as the provider, our good heavenly Father of whom we can ask anything.

The desire is usually expressed as a humble or desperate prayer: "God, *if* you would . . ."

heal
save
move
work
provide

We want to see God glorified in the situation. We desire to see his will done. We are confident that what we are asking for is good, sealed by a sincere faith. But with enough repetition and frustration, with enough times of tripping in the gap, the desire can subtly become the expectation "God, *only if* . . ."

"God, if you would bring the person you have for me" becomes "God, *only if* you bring the person I long for will my life have joy."

"God, if we could have a child" becomes "God, *only if* you give us a child will we have worth as people."

"God, if I could make a difference in this world" becomes "God, *only if* my work makes a difference will my life matter."

"God, if you would heal" becomes "God, *only if* you heal will I trust you."

When desire turns into expectation, our vision of God's goodness becomes defined by the constraints of what we want. Eugene Peterson explained the motive that can develop: "Instead of putting trust in the God who is able to work beyond our expectations, [people] attempt to find a point of leverage at which they can pry a miracle out of God to satisfy what they think they need. Miracle for them has almost nothing to do with God; it is a demand item that will get them what they want."[3]

When it comes to your desires, how do you view God? Is he the five-course steak meal you're hungering for or simply the waiter who brings it out? When we place such expectations and demands on God, we usually package them as conditions in various forms. *Only if* conditions are ossified expectations—sincere desires hardened into stubborn demands—and they blind us to the work God wants to do and is doing, according to *his* wise purposes and good pleasure, not necessarily ours.

THIS AIN'T NEW YORK

Conditions have two parts to them. They start with a protasis ("if . . .") and conclude with an apodosis ("then . . ."). The protasis lays out a certain set of conditions, and the apodosis states the result if they are fulfilled. But don't let a grammar lesson fool you.

Conditions shape the course of our actions and interactions every day, even shaping just about all our relationships. A relationship without conditions means I am committed regardless of what the other person does. The opposite is a conditional or consumer relationship, one that is defined by a certain set of criteria: *If you do what I want or what is to my benefit, then I will stay in the relationship.* That relationship could be with a person or even an organization. I will pay the required cost of membership to continue receiving a benefit. Conditions are how Costco and Lifetime Fitness stay in business.

But conditions can also adversely distort a relationship. Think of how a marriage is affected when conditions begin to define the ways of relating. Instead of unconditional vows like "I choose you in sickness and in health, for richer or poorer," conditions distort the relationship into "as long as you make me happy" or "*only if* you don't . . .*"* The protasis of my desires dictates the apodosis of what I'm willing to put into the relationship. Forgiveness becomes finger-pointing and conditional on the other person's accepting responsibility.

Conditions also distort your relationship with God. Counselor Dr. Bill Clark described how this works through a simple illustration. We might be in some present circumstance (A) with an eye to a preferred future (B) that we have prayed about. As the desire for (B) turns into expectation, we begin to believe that God's eternal resources and purposes are meant to take us there. We even read Scripture and seek counsel that supports our belief that we're supposed to end up at (B).

Dr. Clark asked: "What if God is not as interested in taking us from (A) to (B)? Rather, what if God is working in our lives to take us to (B')?"[4]

If math variables aren't your thing, think about a travel illustration. Imagine God as an airline you are trusting to take you from your current location, say, Miami, to another destination, New York. You pray about New York, study up on it, and talk to people about it. You consult Tripadvisor about things to do there. You get a cool Airbnb in Chelsea. You even score some tickets to *Hamilton*. You are excited about New York, and you expect to step off that plane in LaGuardia.

Then you get off the plane and realize you are not where you thought you would be. Instead of seeing the city skyline, you see mountains. Instead of being in the city that never sleeps, you have to fight to stay awake. It turns out that God wanted to take you to some destination other than New York.

What will you do? You could wallow in disappointment and sadness. You could try to force the issue. You could even try to take matters into your own hands and hitchhike there. You could double down on your conditions and demand that God take you to New York because that is what is fair, what you agreed to. Look carefully enough, and you will find that an *only if* condition is motivating each of those responses.

In fact, the more determined you are to get to the destination you expect, the stronger your *only if* conditions will be. And the stronger your *only if* conditions, the greater the disappointment if God chooses to do something different. You will miss the beauty and opportunity of what God could have for you at a destination you did not expect. The potential for life at your new location will be lost amid the frustration and disappointment of being stuck in a place you did not choose.

And when you can't see the potential of where you are, your *only if* conditions will just get stronger. Conditions can't deal with disappointment without dishing out some sort of punishment. Sometimes that punishment looks like anger and cynicism. Sometimes you develop a critical and judgmental attitude. You might grasp your plans a little tighter in the hope of guaranteeing the outcome.

Only if conditions have several additional side effects that can harden us. The first is that they drive us to comparison, especially as we perceive others moving toward the destination we had hoped for. Comparison then reinforces our *only if*s as we expect God to do for us what he did for those people. "*Only if* you do for me what you did for them will I have worth."

You never win the game of comparison. The outcome is always a skewed picture of reality. Either you will think that you're doing better than your competitor and be filled with a sense of pride and self-righteousness—what the apostle Paul called "vain conceit" (Philippians 2:3, NIV)—or you will think that someone is doing better and beat yourself up in self-pity. Both scenarios ignore what God says about you: you are worse than you think you are (exposing your self-righteousness) but more loved and valued than you could ever imagine (confronting your self-pity).[5]

Related to this, conditions can also lead to shame. In her book *Unashamed,* Heather Nelson explained how our *only if*s are a way to become who we think we should be. Consequently, our worth comes from our ongoing ability to fulfill the conditions we believe will make us loved or accepted.[6] *Only if*s become a kind of rule of life, the measuring stick by which we judge whether we are worthy of love.

"*Only if* I have well-behaved kids will I be worthy of respect."

"*Only if* I am accepted into the right social circles will I be loved and known."

"*Only if* I get married will I have worth in my church."

With every *only if* that we fail to live up to, we feel the shame of not being enough, of not measuring up to God's standard for us—when it's actually our standards that we have put on God.

The most tragic effect of conditions is that you can lose confidence and trust in the One who is actually accomplishing his purposes in your life, just not in the ways you expect. Unfulfilled conditions could lead you to the conclusion that God doesn't know what he's doing, that he can't be trusted. You will be tempted to take matters into your own hands. You will grow impatient and make rash decisions. You will compromise convictions in order to bring about what you desire, even settling for something close to but not quite what you hoped for. In essence, you will be your own god.

ONLY IF ISN'T THE ONLY WAY

Only if conditions are not just a current-day struggle. Shadrach, Meshach, and Abednego could have been ruled by conditions. "*Only if* you preserve our city and provide for us will we be devoted to you." The sad irony is that, for most of their relationship, the people of God held conditions like this over God, but they never kept up their end of the deal. That's what caused God to hand them over.

But when facing the fire, Shadrach, Meshach, and Abednego declared, "*Even if* he does not, we will not worship any other." They chose an *even if* declaration instead of an *only if* condition.

And their story is not the only one. Job was a successful man by every measure. Lots of possessions, ten children, and a deep faith—all his desires had been fulfilled. It would be natural to assume that was why he loved God. All his conditions had been met and exceeded.

Job's story presses on that assumption. The narrative starts with the accuser coming before God and raising this question: "Does Job fear God for no reason? Have you not put a hedge around him and his house and all that he has, on every side? You have blessed the work of his hands, and his possessions have increased in the land. But stretch out your hand and touch all that he has, and he will curse you to your face" (Job 1:9–11). In other words, the accuser suggested that Job was devoted to God only because of the way in which God had fulfilled his conditions. His children, his wealth, even his blamelessness were all the result of satisfied *only if*s. Remove that, and we will see who Job really is.

Job faced the most severe upheaval of conditions imaginable.

The children died (all in one day), the wealth evaporated (in fact, it was stolen or burned), and Job's life came crashing down. His response was just as unpredictable as the circumstances that took his family and wealth: "Job arose and tore his robe and shaved his head and fell on the ground and worshiped. And he said, 'Naked I came from my mother's womb, and naked shall I return. The LORD gave, and the LORD has taken away; blessed be the name of the LORD.' In all this Job did not sin or charge God with wrong" (verses 20–22).

I have a hard time understanding his response. Job was not unaffected by these tragedies. An *even if* life doesn't mean we just put on a happy face and pretend that suffering isn't really all that bad (counterfeit resolve). Job tore his robe and shaved his head, the ancient Near Eastern expression of intense mourning and grief.

Job's statement "Naked I came from my mother's womb, and naked shall I return" could be interpreted as a desperate admission of his state. While recognizing he came into the world with nothing, Job realized he would die that way. I imagine that he wanted to die sooner rather than later.

Yet "Job did not sin or charge God with wrong" (verse 22). He blessed his name. In essence, he recommitted himself to God, acknowledging and trusting in God's provision from the first day of his life until the last. Without using the two words, he made a painful *even if* declaration.

Although Job had already gone through more than one person could ever be expected to endure, that was not the end of his sufferings. The accuser returned and suggested that Job's response wasn't really an expression of *even if* devotion; rather, his conditions ran deeper than children or possessions: "Skin for skin! All that a man has he will give for his life. But stretch out your hand and touch his bone and his flesh, and he will curse you to your face" (2:4–5). Afflict him with sickness, and we will see that all his devotion to God is built on the condition of his own physical well-being.

So Job went through the ringer again as loathsome sores covered his body like an unwelcome body tattoo. As he sat in the figurative and literal ashes of his life, he scraped the scabs and puss off his flesh. His own wife told him to acknowledge the tragic conditions of his life, to curse God and die.

Job's response was an *even if* declaration in question form: "'Shall we receive good from God, and shall we not receive evil?' In all this Job did not sin with his lips" (verse 10). From the narrator's explanation, we know that Job wasn't offering a sinful complaint.

The context tells us that Job wasn't just shrugging his shoulders. No, he expressed what Philip Yancey described as "ambidextrous faith": faith that holds in one hand suffering and unfulfilled expectations and in the other a resolute belief that even now God is at work.[7] Ambidextrous faith gives no authority to the conditions that declare life must unfold in a prescribed way. Ambidextrous faith is the womb of the *even if* life.

ENTER THE *ONLY IF* WITNESSES

The rest of the book of Job walks us through the nuances of Job's *even if* declaration. Job demonstrated the resolve to live an *even if* life especially when his friends and neighbors were all too willing to point out his failures. Job's resolve ebbed and flowed; he believed and doubted. What started out as his friends sitting with him silently for a week took a curious turn as they tried to convince him that he must have failed to meet a divine condition.

The shift is an important one. Instead of one accuser suggesting to God that Job's loyalty was based on God having met Job's conditions, now we get several accusers suggesting to Job that his tragic life was the result of having failed to meet God's. Surely Job must have sinned, or his children must have sinned.

In similar fashion, well-meaning people will offer explanations of our suffering and disappointments. In his book on prayer, Pete Greig described the checklist-like conditions that are offered, especially to explain unanswered prayer: "When [people] hear that my wife is sick, they urge me, with extraordinary levels of eye contact, to pray for her in some better way, or to break off some random curse, or to have her repent of a particular attitude, or to take a particular nutritional supplement, or to visit a particular healing ministry, or to stand on our heads with a garlic clove in each ear, singing the 'Hallelujah Chorus.'"[8]

Each of these pieces of advice is a suggested condition for appeasing God and getting what you desire. Not only do conditions like these fail to account for the complexity and uncertainty of life; they also oversimplify the mystery of God. Worse yet, they assign to God a set of divine conditions that he holds over the sufferer in question: "Because you didn't . . ." or "If you would just . . ." or "If you do such-and-such . . ."

Conditions like these work off the assumption that life will follow a certain formula and, if you don't get what you were wanting, it is because you didn't follow the formula. Religion, in fact, often operates this way. Keep up your part of the deal, and God will keep up his. When something doesn't go the way the formula predicts, recheck the formula. Figure out where you didn't keep up your end (either by commission or by omission). Go back and meet the condition, and God will then do his part. It's a transactional way to relate to God: God will bless you *only if* you do your part.

How will you fight the onslaught of *only if* conditions, both from the outside and from within? You have to declare *even if* over your *only ifs* by going back to the goodness of God. As you consider the conditions people suggest to you, ask yourself, *What does the goodness of God mean? Is he a tit-for-tat deity who demands I do my part if I want a blessing from him?*

Could it be that we hold tightly to our conditions because we secretly believe that God vindictively holds on to his?

From the grand history of God's relationship with his people, we learn that God actually commits to us before he asks anything of us. In other words, he goes all in before he invites. He saves before he commands. He woos before he instructs. God covenants himself to us as our God and then invites us to be his children.

To be clear, there are conditions that come with being his children. He wants our obedience, our trust, and our loyalty. He wants us to forsake our idols and find life in him. But instead of saying, *"Only if* you obey will I be your God," he declares, "I am your God who has saved you; now you can be my child." He does not withhold himself until we can meet his conditions. He commits to us, even knowing that we will never meet any of his conditions without his help.

HANDING OVER OUR CONDITIONS

The covenantal, compassionate God calls you to release your *only ifs* by trusting him. He knows what he's doing in your life. You are not forgotten. You may not be in the New York City you hoped for, but that doesn't mean that God has left you off the map. It's okay to have expectations, but hold them with an open hand, or better yet, place them in the hands of a good God who is at work even now.

There's one last thing to know about conditions. While it's true that our *only ifs* can be a way of controlling our situations and demanding that God meet our expectations, there is a kind of condition that can humbly submit to God. Instead of an arms-crossed demand, this other kind of condition comes in hands-open dependence. It's the condition of intercession, asking God to intervene in a situation that is desperate and difficult.

In the gospel of Luke, a leper came to Jesus, fell on his face, and said, "Lord, if you will, you can make me clean" (5:12). Lepers were social outcasts to be avoided, the COVID-19 stricken patients of our day, except in a more permanent sense. In desperation, the man fell facedown before the only One who could heal him. He pleaded his case before Jesus with a conditional statement that left the response in God's court. He stated his desire, even made known his need, and then put himself at the mercy of God.

"If it's your will, you can heal." It echoes the same confidence we have seen in Shadrach, Meshach, and Abednego: "If he wills, our God can save." There's an open-ended faith in this simple request, a condition suggesting possibility and hope, not demand.

I have heard this condition whispered by a family in the waiting room of the NICU as a baby is delivered at twenty-three weeks. I have prayed this condition with the broken spouse of an alcoholic whose life is imploding a bit more each day, taking loved ones out with him. I have even exchanged this condition via text messages while a friend is about to interview for a job he needs.

Believe me, there is no sense of arrogant control in these prayers. They're altogether different from the *only if* conditions described above. Rather, they're the helpless, desperate, humble prayers of worshippers who are preparing to embrace an *even if* declaration.

"If you will . . . you can . . ." But *even if* you do not, we will continue to pray. We will continue to look to you because you're all we have, God. We will continue to trust in your kind care for us and all those we love *even if* you do not do it in the way that we are asking.

The power of the *even if* life is that while we continue to pray with fervency and ask according to our desires, at the same time we declare our trust that God is sovereign and will be good. Our devotion is not determined by how God answers our prayers as much as it is formed by the character of the God to whom we pray. He alone is wise. He alone is good. We can trust him.

We see the culminating example of *even if* devotion on the night Jesus was betrayed. He traveled with some of his disciples to the Garden of Gethsemane and poured his heart out. He looked over his shoulder and saw that his emotional support system, his disciples, couldn't even stay awake. And he felt the fresh pain of being stabbed in the back by one of his disciples.

Then, the worst of it all, he anticipated the abandonment that he would feel on the cross—a temporary and unthinkable split between Father and Son as Jesus took on the sins of the world. It would be suffering worse than the crucifixion itself.

As the leper came before Jesus, so Jesus offered his own condition: "Father, if you are willing, remove this cup from me" (Luke 22:42). Jesus asked the Father to remove the cup, to figure out a different way, to pass it on. But unlike Jesus's answer to the leper's request—"I will; be clean" (5:13)—the Father, in his sovereignty, would not remove the cup. Jesus would become unclean like a leper, taking on the sins of the world in a public demonstration of God's mercy and justice. The sacrificial lamb must go to the cross.

And Jesus declared his own *even if:* "Nevertheless, not my will, but yours, be done" (22:42). *Even if* you will not remove this cup, your will must be done, not mine. Jesus submitted his desires to the Father's will, believing that God's will is perfect and his ways are good. Jesus's *even if* declaration was an act of humility to the point of death, even death on a cross (Philippians 2:8).

That means you don't have to hold on to your *only if*s as a way of establishing your identity and worth. The cost Jesus paid on the cross says you are valuable enough to die for. It means you don't have to hide in shame. It means every condition that God might have had has been fulfilled by Jesus, and now his Spirit lives in you.

Securing your future is no longer your burden to bear. God is trustworthy. No matter how hard or foreign the road right in front of you might seem, the Cross reminds you of the lengths God will go to in order to save you and keep you. He will not forsake you now.

George Everett Ross summed up what faith looks like when we release our *only ifs*. The encouragement we receive from Job's *even if* beautifully points us to Jesus:

I have come to understand that there are two kinds of faith. One says if and the other says though. One says: "If everything goes well, if my life is prosperous, if I'm happy, if no one I love dies, if I'm successful, then I will believe in God and say my prayers and go to the church and give what I can afford." The other says though: though the cause of evil prosper, though I sweat in Gethsemane, though I must drink my cup at Calvary— nevertheless, precisely then, I will trust the Lord who made me. So Job cries: "Though he slay me, yet will I trust Him."[9]

5

Fake It till You Make It

In the late 1990s, Gwyneth Paltrow starred in an English romantic drama called *Sliding Doors*. After being fired from her job, Helen (Paltrow's character) heads home dejected, seeking the comfort of her live-in boyfriend, Gerry, who, unbeknownst to her, is having an affair. She catches her boyfriend in bed with the other woman, and this begins a sequence of events in which Helen sets out on her own, finds her true self, and experiences newfound love.

Honestly, it's a pretty predictable story line. Hero(ine) experiences heartbreak. Hero(ine) finds himself or herself, finds love along the way, and lives happily ever after. Throw in a witty best friend, a moment of tension when it all goes wrong, some underestimated ability that a charming stranger (future love interest) coaxes out, and the movie is just like every other in its genre.

What makes *Sliding Doors* unique is that the movie actually explores two plotlines diverging from one seemingly insignificant moment—whether or not Helen actually catches the train home. Just after Helen barely misses the train, the movie rewinds ten seconds and imagines what would have happened if she had caught the train.

From this point, two alternate realities play out side by side. In one reality, Helen gets home late, fails to catch her cheating boyfriend in the act, and lives under the constant deceptions of her unfaithful lover. Frustrated, we follow a weary Helen, who has no idea how much she is playing the fool, working two waitressing jobs and unknowingly supporting her cheating boyfriend's shenanigans.

In the other, Helen arrives home to find Gerry in bed with another woman, promptly leaves him, cuts her hair short (because that's apparently what women do after a bad breakup), and proceeds to step out on her own, following the archetypal narrative that makes us all love (or hate) movies in this genre.[1]

The movie creatively depicts something all of us wrestle with at some point—the *if onlys* of another life we could have lived. This is the second *counter if* that we might encounter as we mind the gap between what we thought life would be and how it actually turned out.

That frustration is what the actor Philip Seymour Hoffman expressed two years before his untimely death. In an interview about his role as Willy Loman, the main character in Arthur Miller's *Death of a Salesman,* he explained the universal appeal of the seventy-year-old Broadway show: "The idea that you have a vision of what you're supposed to be, or going to be, or where your kids are going to be—and that that doesn't work out—is always going to be something that's going to affect people and move people."[2] Everyone wrestles with what could have been versus what is. There's that pesky gap again.

No matter how successful or according-to-plan life might seem, we all wonder, *What would have happened if I had made a different choice?* Sometimes we wonder out of curiosity, our imaginations whimsically playing out a variety of hypothetical scenarios. *What if I had gone to another college? What if I were in another line of work? How would life be different if I had married a different person?*

My kids go through these mental gymnastics even moments after they choose one treat over another, imagining what would have happened had they chosen the ice cream instead of the cookie. In other more punitive moments, what would have happened had they listened to Mom instead of goofing off?

When life disappoints, the wondering can be more serious, welling up from painful longings for a life we wish were different in significant ways.

> *What would have happened had I chosen a different spouse, one that didn't cheat on me?*
> *How would my life be different had I not made that mistake?*
> *What if I were married by now?*
> *What if my pregnancy had been full term?*
> *What if the car hadn't swerved off the road?*
> *What if the test results had been different? If Mom or Dad were still here?*

These wonderings lead to the lingering thought *If only something had been different.* Whether you're in remorse over a past failure or dreaming of a different present, *if onlys* grow from dissatisfaction with where you are currently. In that way, they, too, emerge from the unfulfilled desires that give rise to our *only if* conditions. The difference is that while *only ifs* are desires turned demands, *if onlys* are desires expressed as regrets. *If onlys* have just as much paralyzing power, leaving us resigned that nothing will ever change—not our identities or our lots in life.

NOBODY KNOWS THE TROUBLE I'VE SEEN

If only regrets come from the way you look at your mistakes and failures. You might be haunted by mistakes, a broken past that you can't seem to shake or outrun. You have memories that you are not proud of—harsh words that you wish you could take back, broken relationships that you would have handled differently, moments of anger or self-centeredness that hurt someone deeply. There are decisions you wish you could do over and choices you wish you could unmake.

All of us have these regrets lying deep in our hearts that end up motivating us and influencing our behaviors in ways we're not always aware. I served with an incredible woman named Mary, who was active in the church and infectious in her faith. She poured her life into high school girls, taking late-night calls and giving so much of her time to discipling them. She basically set up a counseling office at the local Panera. We met regularly so I could get an update on her ministry.

At one meeting, she informed me that she was stepping away. "I can't do this anymore," she confessed as tears began to flow from her eyes.

"What happened? What do you mean?" I was blindsided. She was one of my best leaders.

"I feel like I am living two lives."

Dread came over me as my imagination conjured a thousand scenarios of inappropriate behavior. I admit that, instead of thinking about how to minister to her, I became preoccupied with how to clean up whatever she was about to say.

"I'm carrying a terrible secret from my past. I'm so tired of living under the shame and hypocrisy of what I've done."

She shared how before she met Christ while in college, she had been sexually active with her boyfriend. She got pregnant and was persuaded to abort the baby. It was a *dark* secret that she had carried with her for more than a decade. She had never told anyone, and the guilt was unbearable.

As she shared her story, the question that unlocked the desires of her heart was a simple one: "Do you believe that God has forgiven you, or do you believe that while saving you, he still holds this over you?" Over the ensuing conversation, it became clear to both of us that so much of her service in the church flowed from the deep desire to make up for her past.

It didn't make her love for her girls any less genuine or her ministry to them any less sincere. Rather, she was motivated by a complex mix of love for them and regret. Perhaps by helping some girls avoid the mistakes that she had made, she could rid herself of her guilt and shame. In a weird way, we realized this might be an attempt to serve out a sentence of her own making.

But it only made it worse. Unbeknownst to both of us, she was keeping a subconscious ledger, counting hours of time served, lives changed, and text messages sent, to try to balance out the regret of her mistake. And if she ever dropped the ball and failed her girls? The regret would intensify. Her inner voice would condemn her: "Not only have you taken the life of a baby, but now you can't even make it right when given the chance! You're hopeless." The self-accusation was too loud to quiet anymore. The burden of guilty regret was too much. She wanted to quit.

By the end of our conversation, we were both reminded of our need for God. As I counseled her, I realized that I had my own ledger. Regrets shaped so much of my leadership and ways of relating. We were in tears as we believed afresh the promise of God—that our ledgers could never be balanced by our own efforts. Only Jesus could do it, and he joyfully and lovingly did.

Regret, while a suitable motivator for repentance, is an insatiable rationale for good deeds. When you serve, work, wed, or parent out of regret, you're on the pathway to burnout and disappointment because you never know whether you've done enough.

There's no exchange rate to calculate how many and what kinds of good deeds will pay for mistakes. Just when you think you've settled your debt, you discover that there's another list of demands on the next page.

To approach regrets this way is to live with a functionally karmic view of life. Not only are you required to balance the scales with your good works; you also get what you deserve. If you mess up, then you deserve the fire of the furnace. When life takes a hard turn, regrets tell you that you deserve the hardship—divine retribution for past sins. The best you can do is to accept it and try to make up for it with the chances you have now.

You might think, *God won't bless me anymore until I can make it up to him. So I can't ask him to remove this hardship.* The shame of your past compounds regret, making you think that you are forever defined by your mistakes and that your only hope is not to mess things up further.

This can lead to great passivity. Parents living under regrets give up intentionally parenting their kids. I knew a mom who refused to take ownership for discipling her sons because of the guilt of her failed marriages and relationships. She secretly believed that because of her mistakes, she had no rightful authority to encourage her kids to godliness. Regret muted her.

Others will work overtime to try to make up for the things they've done. Like with my friend Mary, this response to regret will most often take the form of a vow, some kind of promise to make it right, to turn over a new leaf. In this way, *if only* regrets form an unholy union with the *only if* conditions of our hearts. "*If only* I hadn't messed up like that" leads to "*Only if* I can show how sorry I am and make up for it will I be worthy of love." By our own willpower and conviction, we attempt to prove that we are worthy of blessing. Locked in the prison cell of our mistakes, we work and work until we find the right *only if* key to free ourselves.

Your regrets do not have to define you. You are called to a

higher purpose than just making up for the past. Your past may explain you: regrets might explain why you have a passion for certain causes, or they might give shape to the way you resist temptations. Concerns about not making the same mistakes might explain why you relate to people the way you do and even whom you spend time with. But you are not just the sum of your past choices.

If you are in Christ, you are a new creation (2 Corinthians 5:17). That's your identity. You are the beautiful project of mercy that God had in mind at the Cross. That means that regret can now lead to repentance and restoration instead of condemnation and retribution. "As far as the east is from the west," the psalmist declared, "so far does he remove our transgressions from us" (Psalm 103:12). Those are opposite ends of the spectrum. Just like you and your sins. No *if only* regret can stand against God's grace.

THE GOOD OLD DAYS

A second type of regret is not over a *broken* past but over a *golden* one. Rather than feeling remorse for mistakes and failures, it cherishes "the good old days," a simpler time that you can't get back to. This kind of regret most often shows up as nostalgia.

Nostalgia is different from the dayenu-type remembrance of God's faithfulness. Israel's dayenu recollection led them to remember God's deliverance from Egypt: "To him who struck down the firstborn of Egypt . . . and brought Israel out from among them . . . with a strong hand and an outstretched arm, for his steadfast love endures forever" (Psalm 136:10–12). They praised God for his deliverance and his faithfulness. They were reminded of God's goodness, and their remembrance strengthened their confidence in him.

But in the wilderness, when faced with real troubles and

threats, Israel's nostalgia led them to remember an altogether-different picture of the past: "The whole congregation of the people of Israel grumbled against Moses and Aaron in the wilderness, and the people of Israel said to them, 'Would that we had died by the hand of the LORD in the land of Egypt, when we sat by the meat pots and ate bread to the full, for you have brought us out into this wilderness to kill this whole assembly with hunger'" (Exodus 16:2–3).

Israel faced a scarcity of food in the wilderness, and they succumbed to their fears. In their nostalgia, they actually believed that slavery in Egypt was to be preferred to freedom in the wilderness with God as their provider. Nostalgia made Israel forget that Pharaoh, in his paranoia, killed their sons and subjected them to impossible brick production quotas. In their nostalgic regret, they fooled themselves into remembering a fictional slavery where they sat by meat pots with full stomachs.

Regret over a golden past is fed by discontentment with our present circumstances compared with where we believe we once were. To the degree that we pessimistically look at our situations now, we exaggerate how good it was back then. Brené Brown described this tendency: "Think about how often we compare ourselves and our lives to a memory that nostalgia has so completely edited that it never really existed: 'Remember when . . . ? Those were the days . . . '"[3]

This kind of regret works differently from regret over a broken past. Regret over a broken past makes us want to forget it. Regret over a golden past makes us want to relive it. While we might have remorse over our mistakes, we romanticize the golden past when our devotion was stronger, our bodies more able, our love purer. Romantic notions are fairly harmless until we begin to think that if we could just go back and be like we once were, then God would be pleased. We begin to compare our current lives with the reconstructed nostalgic versions of them.

We do this in our spiritual lives too. We'll read verses like Revelation 2:4–5—"I have this against you, that you have abandoned the love you had at first. Remember therefore from where you have fallen; repent, and do the works you did at first"—and then believe that God is commanding us to return to the golden age of our first love. We long for that purer time when we were fervent believers who memorized every Bible verse, took notes on every sermon, and shared Jesus with every person we met.

However, in those verses, Jesus wasn't calling the church members to relive their "glory years," but rather, he was pointing out how they had lost sight of love in the midst of all their good works. Somewhere along the way, a passion for causes and doctrinal stances outpaced their love for Jesus. In the same way, Jesus isn't calling you to a golden age. He doesn't love the past version of you more than the current you. He's calling you to a true love in the present. In fact, whatever golden period you remember is like imitation gold compared with the new things he wants to do in you now.

I once counseled a man who kept comparing the faith of his childhood with where he was in his current walk with God. He had a rough upbringing with little stability and a whole lot of poverty. With all that he had going against him, his very life was a miracle. He had made more than his fair share of mistakes, living daily with the ongoing consequences and doing his best not to be defined by them.

Yet he kept coming back to this regret: "*If only* I could have a pure faith like I did when I was a child." Somewhere in his nostalgia, the simple faith he had as a child became the gold standard, the standard that he even believed God held him to. While in some ways that could have been true, what was not true was his belief that if he could just get back to that childhood faith, then God would be pleased with him.

He neglected to see—or at least he minimized—the endurance that his sufferings had forged. He overlooked how he had developed a dependence on God's grace because he knew first-hand how he could destroy his own life and hurt those whom he loved. It wasn't like the dependence he remembered as a child. Though he could see how God had brought him through the wilderness, feeding him with manna all along the way, he couldn't truly celebrate that grace because his faith now was different from the faith he had when he was thirteen.

In short, he was confusing his childhood faith with childlike faith. Childhood faith is a reconstructed memory of yesteryears. Childlike faith is what Jesus calls us to in the present: a humble and simple dependence on God. Jesus doesn't call you to the faith of your childhood. He calls you to trust in the good work he is doing now, with childlike faith that your heavenly Father loves you and cares for you.

Regrets over a broken past and regrets over a golden past both keep us from seeing the work that God has done and is continuing to do right now. They fix our eyes on freeze-frame stills of the past that we then either run from or run to. We end up missing the beauty of present grace—grace that the hymn "Amazing Grace" so richly captures:

> Through many dangers, toils, and snares,
> I have already come.
> 'Tis grace has brought me safe thus far,
> And grace will lead me home.[4]

God has grace for your regrets, grace that has been working in your life to bring you thus far. God's grace gives you the new start you're longing for by settling the balance sheet once and for all. You're no longer in the red. Bryan Stevenson, in his compelling call for justice and mercy, summed it up: "Each of us is more than the worst thing we've ever done."[5] God's grace, given through the sacrificial death of Jesus, covers your sins. Receive it afresh now. Let it transform your present and lead you into a future that will be far better than your golden past ever was.

I COULD HAVE BEEN SOMEBODY

Before we speak an *even if* declaration over our regrets, we need to talk about one more kind of regret, perhaps the most daunting of them all. This kind of regret is hard to identify, formed by longings for an unrealized present rather than by memories of the past. I call them fantasy regrets because while regrets over the past—broken or golden—deal with actual events (even if they are distorted in our memories), fantasy regrets are shaped by imaginary ones.

Jon Bloom gave some shape to this idea: "We often can't identify the genesis of fantasy regrets because they are amalgamations of various messages, impressions, aspirations, envies, and hopes we've picked up along the way . . . We don't recognize them as fantasies; they just impress us as *the way things should be.*"[6]

Each of us lives by a notion of what life is supposed to be and whom we are supposed to be in it. A number of factors might contribute to this picture: what expectations people put on you, what you were taught to celebrate or value. While your picture might be different from mine, all of us keep a timeline to chart our progress toward that picture. Fantasy regrets come when we don't hit the benchmarks we measure ourselves by.

Life will not always match up to the pictures we imagine, especially along the timelines we track. As we chase the lives we are supposed to be living, we will grow increasingly discontent because the dreams are always just out of reach, never fully realized. Even when you arrive at a particular goal, the fantasy regrets linger. Have you ever reached a certain milestone, yet—whether by comparison or some other self-accusing voice—you still think, *By this stage of my life, I should have done more?*

In September 2016, I was installed as the lead pastor of my church. (*Installed*. Like an appliance. How's that for a word picture?) It was a beautiful service, filled with tears of gratitude, honoring, baton passing, and recognizing God's grace. Some unique factors made it even more significant. I was being commissioned to lead a majority-culture megachurch as a Korean American. I received the baton from my mentor and dear friend who had pastored the church for more than twenty-five years.

Looking from the outside, most people will conclude, "Wow, what a significant achievement." Yet, not a few days later, in the midst of the afterglow of that powerful gathering, I found myself thinking, *There's [so-and-so], who became the lead pastor of a bigger church at an earlier age. I'd better work hard to catch up and make a difference.*

Are you kidding me? My fantasy regrets tried to condemn me by pointing out what I hadn't achieved, what I still needed to do. There was no time for gratitude for having received from God something so undeserved. No, it was time to prove myself and earn my keep. There's that ledger balancing again.

Fantasy regrets say *"If only . . ."* about what could have or should have been, even as what you imagine might be completely irrational. My inner voice was arguing, "*If only* you had become a lead pastor earlier, then you could make a real contribution."

Pay attention to how you fill in the *if only* regret. It indicates more than just what dissatisfies you. It shows what you're longing for. Your *if onlys* describe your version of paradise and sometimes even how you imagine you will get there.

The stressed-out mom thinks, *If only I had a little more time or more obedient children,* to deal with the self-condemnation of not being the perfect parent.

If only I could lose a couple more pounds is the longing of the self-conscious person whose worth is determined by the scale.

The single person wishes, *If only I were married,* because marriage is the means by which acceptance and intimacy will be found.

*If only*s reveal what you're looking to for salvation. Peel away the layers of your *if only* wish, and you'll find the would-be savior that is offering to bring about the perfect world (or version of you).

IT'S NOT YOU; IT'S ME

As I've already hinted, fantasy regrets don't just pop up from our imaginations. They sprout from the seedlings of what we see around us. One of my favorite parts in the book *The Boy, the Mole, the Fox and the Horse* is a short interchange between the boy and the mole.

The boy asks his new friend, "What do you think is the biggest waste of time?" The mole responds, "Comparing yourself to others."[7]

We've already talked about how you never win the game of comparison, but let me add one more important observation. Fantasy regrets feed off comparison. Think about how the highlight reels of social media cause you to imagine what your life could look like by reminding you of what it isn't. You get daily newsfeeds illustrating all the things that are out there, the things you are missing out on.

Pictures of amazing meals, descriptions of cool adventures in exotic destinations, boasts about accomplishments, and swoonings about intimate relationships taunt us into thinking, *What am I doing with my life?* Pinterest boards become the aggregated reminders of all the ways our lives don't measure up and just aren't very interesting. We begin to regret our lives as we desire others. "*If only . . .*"

The COVID-19 quarantine brought this into even more aggravating focus. As we sat at home, isolated and grieving the loss of normalcy, we watched as people posted the amazing work their homeschooling kids were accomplishing, the amazing meals they were whipping up from what was in their pantries, or the incredible new hobby of gardening they were taking up. *If only I had the creativity and ingenuity to do something like that. If only my kids were obedient like that. If only I had the resolve to redeem the time by doing a house project like that.*

What we long for or imagine can even form an unholy pairing with our regrets over the past. Our *if onlys* amplify the regret that things turned out the way they did, intensifying the disappointment that they didn't go the way we imagined. We then regret that we didn't do more (or less) to change our present situations.

I'll share one more illustration as to how comparisons feed our *if only* regrets. Superman is a beloved comic book superhero. He is noble, powerful, and unbeatable. What most people don't know is that Superman had a supervillain alternate version of himself named Bizarro. Bizarro was like Superman in strength and abilities but was his negative image in just about everything else. He opposed all that Superman stood for.

My life often feels like a battle between Bizarro and Superman. I am very familiar with the Superman version of me. The Superman version of me has achieved so much. He never loses his temper with his kids and always has the right answer for every situation that he faces. He rises early and goes to bed late, always thinks about how to sacrifice himself for his bride. Superman Mitchel is an incredible lover and a faithful friend, is handy around the house, and crushes his weekly goals every time. He is the pastor of a thriving church, an accomplished author, a respected scholar, and a trusted community leader. He never fails anyone. The Superman version of me is amazing.

And a jerk. He's a jerk because, even while not doing it intentionally, he makes the real Bizarro version of me feel like a disappointment, a failed project, a remedial sinner who just needs a lot of help today. The Bizarro version of me is constantly afraid of being found out—that people will realize that he's only playing the part of Superman. The Bizarro version of me can't compete. Like a younger brother who's always getting pummeled by his older sibling but continues to pick fights, Bizarro me keeps going head to head with Superman and losing every time. Superman me makes me miserable.

Brennan Manning has a less geeky way of describing Superman. He calls him the impostor self.[8] The impostor self is the person you think you should be but know you aren't, the embodiment of fantasy and past regrets. The impostor self has to present the appearance of having it together so that he will be admired. Everything about the impostor is superficial and external. What others see is a well-manicured, manufactured version of who we think we should be, the result of our constant attempts to make our *if onlys* reality.

In actuality, the impostor self lives in fear of disapproval and thus is preoccupied with acceptance and achievement. The impostor self is defined by what she does, constantly spending inordinate amounts of energy surveying and maintaining her facade in order to make sure no one can see the real her. The fear of being found out is a driving force. Yet, maybe because of all the energy required to put up the facade, the impostor demands to be noticed. After all, approval comes only from recognition.

The impostor can't ever experience real intimacy, because the level to which a person is known is the level to which he is loved. The real self is buried beneath layers of pretending and presenting. Thus, any connection we have with others comes as they relate to and like the carefully curated version of ourselves.

The result is that we don't let people know us deeply. And this isn't true just at the interpersonal level; the impostor self even shapes the way we relate to God. We can live out of the impostor self for so long that not only do we believe that people around us accept only the impostor version but we also begin to believe that God himself loves only the impostor.

Stay in this way of being long enough, and the impostor self becomes an impostor life. The suffocating burden of the impostor self is that we constantly compare our real lives with the fantasy ones, all the while believing that others are comparing us with those impostor lives too.

Much of the impostor self is formed by the way we handle our regrets—both real and imagined. The impostor self is the one who will make up for or cover up the past. That perfect person will make us worthy. In a classic misdirection ploy, the reasoning goes that if you can show the world how good you're doing now, no one will notice your broken past.

Or when our lots in life don't measure up to the ones that we imagine, we expend ourselves trying to pretend that we've achieved more than we actually have. We work extra hard to present the facade of having it all together. We will do whatever we can to live the lives that we believe will make us worthy of love and acceptance, even if we have to fake it.

The tragedy of trying to live out of the impostor self is that we'll inevitably fail. We'll never fully attain the lives we envision, because they're imaginary. The bits and pieces we string together won't line up, and we'll constantly live in fear of being found out. We will beat ourselves up with regrets and fantastical wishes, all because we think that the impostor self is the normative one and that our current realities are just poor, distorted showings, reminding us of what our lives should have been.

What does your impostor self look like today? What has the impostor version of you achieved? What are his or her character traits? One way you can know when you are living in the shadow of your impostor self is when you find yourself using words like

should and *by now. I should have made that promotion by now. I
should be doing more. I should be married by now. We should be
homeowners by now. I should be past this by now. I should have
figured it out by now. I should be over that habitual sin by now.*
The conclusion to these kinds of thoughts is *I'm not good
enough*—a portfolio of reasons that the impostor version of you is
better.

These phrases form thought habits that cause us to cower before the impostor self. We have to rescript our inner monologue
by breaking this pattern of thinking. The next time you find yourself thinking, *I should . . . by now,* ask a follow-up question:
"Compared with whom?" Or if you like talking to yourself in a
more in-your-face tone: "Says who?"

Expose the basis of your comparison, and you might discover
that the only person comparing your real self to the imaginary
you is you.

WHOM GOD COMPARES YOU WITH

Years ago, I had the joy of leading a graduating high school senior
to faith in Jesus. It happened in a nonchalant manner over a slice
of pie at a local bakery. The waitress would never have suspected
that heaven came down and an eternity was irrevocably altered as
angels rejoiced over that little booth in Wheaton, Illinois.

Seeing people's burdens lifted as they realize and respond to
the truth that Jesus has taken their burdens on himself is something I will never get bored with. This young man's newfound life
started with the characteristic excitement of one who has been
forgiven. He would, however, constantly get down on himself for
not being further along than he was.

As a bright man who graduated at the top of his class, he had
great expectations for what he could achieve, and this applied to
his new spiritual life as well. He didn't know enough about the

Bible. He wasn't disciplined enough to pray. He didn't know how churches worked. His expectations for himself were unfairly high because he was comparing himself with the super-Christian version of himself. His impostor self was far more mature than his real self even after just a few months of intentional discipleship.

After one particularly intense discussion about the Bible, his frustrations couldn't be contained.

"I should know that by now," he chided himself.

"Says who?" I asked.

"I feel like I've wasted so much time." (He was only seventeen.)

"Bro, you've got time. God called you and saved you according to his timetable. You can't mess that up—and you haven't."

"I just feel like I'm supposed to know more and be further along."

I wanted to warn him, "If you feel that way now, wait until God starts showing you sin patterns and thoughts in your heart." But I held my tongue. I didn't want to overwhelm my young disciple.

He then compared himself with other Christians his age who had come to faith earlier, and he condemned himself. He even began to think that God was disappointed with his rate of growth, impatiently demanding that he know more and do more (like the impostor version of himself was doing). These thought patterns threatened to steal the joy of his newfound faith.

The enormous mountain of all that he *wasn't* overshadowed God's goodness in pursuing him and saving him. Like a dense fog, the *if onlys* of his nascent discipleship journey threatened to wipe out his view of God's mercy. He couldn't ever keep up with his impostor self. The hurts of his past accused him—how could God ever use someone who was so far behind everyone else?

The sobering, corrective salve of God's Word came from the unlikeliest of places to refocus my young friend: "Only let us hold true to what we have attained" (Philippians 3:16). It's a verse that's tucked right behind Paul's magisterial declaration about pressing on, forgetting what lies behind and straining toward what is ahead (verses 12–14). Paul encouraged the Philippians to remember that while they may have a way to go, God was calling them to live in faithfulness where they were now.

God used that small verse to remind us both to be faithful and obedient to what God was showing us now. We were able to confront his fantasy regrets—the *if only* comparisons with his imaginary self, who had become a Christian long before and had experienced God in deeper ways than he could ever. Who was telling him where he should be by now? Who was setting the timetable for his growth? Who had created the spiritual growth curve that he was comparing himself with? How did he know he was in the bottom percentile? Was God saying that? We exposed the lie for what it was. The one holding a timetable and growth curve over my friend was the impostor version of himself.

In thinking more about this subtle struggle we face, I've come to realize that the pressure to be where we think we should be is different from the ambition to grow and become something better. In the latter, there's a drive that God's sanctifying work in us should produce. It's what Paul described when he said, "I press on toward the goal for the prize of the upward call of God in Christ Jesus" (verse 14). Paul had a desire to know Christ, to become like him in his suffering, and to attain the resurrection of the dead (verses 10–11). He wasn't there yet, so he made it his aim. This kind of ambition is good, grounded in hope and glory, flowing from the belief that God's grace will bear fruit in our lives.

In contrast, *if only* regrets try to motivate by comparisons that shout, "You are never good enough, never accomplished enough, but you should be. So get to work." *If only* regrets presume that we should have it all together and that because we don't, we are colossal failures. And in that way, they subtly deny what God actually says about us—we are helpless and prone to wander, reck-lessly pursuing what will lead to our demise. Even our imagined selves are not sufficient to earn God's approval without the work of Jesus on our behalf.

Philippians 3:16 invites us to consider where we are now, not compared with where we think we should be or even where oth-ers think we should be by now. Rather, Paul called us to ask the question "Where am I really?" As Mark Buchanan put it, "By re-imagining our lives . . . I don't mean the reverie of an 'Ah, if only . . .' What I mean is that we see our lives in their truest light: see them for what they truly are, and know what really matters, and what doesn't."[9]

If you'll see your life in the truest light, you'll realize a sobering truth. God won't compare the real you with the impostor you, because the impostor version of you doesn't exist. God knows only true things. That means when you feel guilty before God because you haven't measured up to your imagined self, when you confess, "God, I'm sorry that I haven't learned that by now. I should be further along," God says, "Compared with whom? Who is this person you're comparing yourself with?"

Thomas Merton explained it in more eloquent detail: "[The impostor self] is the man that I want myself to be but who cannot exist, because God does not know anything about him. . . . My false and private self is the one who wants to exist outside the reach of God's will and God's love—outside of reality and outside of life. And such a self cannot help but be an illusion."[10]

And here's the truth that can set you free: the place where you find yourself now, the place that seems so unpleasant compared with where you should be, is exactly where God wants to meet you with his grace. You can't ever be your imagined self, and you don't want to be either because even your impostor version falls short. In fact, that's why God doesn't compare you with your imagined self. He compares you with Christ. And if you think that there's a wide gap between you and your impostor, Jesus is in a different universe in terms of his perfection.

The good news is that God knows we can never be like Jesus without his ongoing intervention. On top of that, Jesus died in your place so that you could have his perfection. Through the Cross, he exposes our fantasy notions that *if only* we could be our imaginary selves, then we would be loved. He invites us to crucify our imaginary selves and to instead receive real grace for our real state so that we can become what God really wants us to be as the reflection of his Son.

This is how we call out our *if onlys* for what they are. We choose to believe that God desires to give us what we need for where we really are. *If onlys* come from what we wish for, and that is altogether different from hope. Wishful thinking leads to regret. Hope leads to resolve founded on the promises of God.

WHEN *IF ONLY* BECOMES *EVEN IF*

The way to declare *even if* over your *if onlys* is to identify and name your regrets. You won't be able to avoid feeling regret, but you will find that in naming your regrets and going to God, he will meet you with what you need.

In John 11, Jesus had a touching interchange with three siblings who were his dear friends. Jesus cared deeply for Mary, Martha, and their brother, Lazarus. Yet when Lazarus fell sick, Jesus delayed in visiting him. Four days after Lazarus died, Jesus finally reached Bethany, and Martha came out to meet him as he approached the house. Mary was too distraught (perhaps even disappointed that Jesus had taken so long?), so she stayed at home.

Martha stated her *if only* regret: "Lord, if [only] you had been here, my brother would not have died" (verse 21). Mary would eventually come out and say the same thing but with more passion. Falling at his feet, she cried, "Lord, if [only] you had been here, my brother would not have died" (verse 32). *If only* the One who could heal strangers just by saying the word or by having them touch his garment had come in time to heal his friend.

Martha named her regret, but she didn't stop there. "But even now I know that whatever you ask from God, God will give you" (verse 22). Regret gave way to confidence and belief with a dash of resolve thrown in. Don't miss the subtle whisper of an *even if* declaration: "*Even if* death looks like the final verdict, I put my trust in you."

Martha wasn't even thinking immediate resurrection. The ensuing dialogue with Jesus shows that she had no expectation that Jesus would raise Lazarus except at the end of ends. All she could do was acknowledge that she trusted Jesus's power and what he could have done. Then Jesus did the unthinkable with her regret. He raised her brother from the dead.

Like Martha's and Mary's, our *if only* regrets can highlight our ultimate desire for the God who alone can truly save. We long for the One who can save us from our broken pasts and who can make something better of our lives than even the nostalgic, romanticized versions we often settle for. As we face our regrets, we can learn to declare *even if* by putting our confidence in the goodness of God, who saved us from our own ruin at great cost to himself.

Make this declaration: "*Even if* my life doesn't measure up to the one I imagined, *even if* I bear the consequences of a past I have been forgiven of, *even if* the good things God has done for me are only memories . . . I will worship the One who has forgiven, the One who is for me and withholds no good thing from me, the One who will always be good."

Put your regrets in their place through your *even if* declaration. Strip them of their power by naming your sins and believing that Jesus died for them. "*Even if* my past can't be undone, I will worship you, God, because you have cleansed me and forgiven me. I need your mercy to protect me from making the same mistakes again."

You can thank God for your golden past and believe in his goodness to you right now. Gratefully declare, "*Even if* I never come close to the golden years again, I will worship you, God, because you can do even more than what you did before."

Call out your imagined, impostor self: "*Even if* I lose every battle to my impostor self, I will worship you, God, because Jesus loved and died for the real me, the real me that he will form into his image."

The prophet Isaiah encouraged the people of Israel after a time of judgment:

> Remember not the former things,
>   nor consider the things of old.
> Behold, I am doing a new thing;
>   now it springs forth, do you not perceive it?
> I will make a way in the wilderness
>   and rivers in the desert. (Isaiah 43:18–19)

God calls us out of the past, out of the imaginary, into a reality that he is creating, a reality in which he is fulfilling his greater promises of redemption and restoration. As we believe this, we say, "*Even if* life doesn't look like what it was in the past, *even if* what I imagine never comes to be, I will trust in the goodness of the God who has brought me here and has not forgotten me. I will trust the God who is doing a new thing."

6

Control Freaks of the World . . . Unite
(in Carefully Thought-Out, Appropriate Ways)

Take a deep breath. We've dog-paddled through some deep waters, examining the *counter if*s that can keep us from living the *even if* life: the *only if* conditions we place on God, demanding he do our will; and the *if only* regrets that keep us stuck in the past or chained to a fictional version of ourselves, blinding us to the new work that God is doing all around us.

The *even if* declaration calls us to remember God's goodness and to resolve to worship him, especially when life doesn't make sense. We remember his faithfulness, his unchanging character, and his good purposes for our lives. In spite of conditions unfulfilled and regrets that might still linger, we say, "*Even if* it isn't what I expected or wanted, I will worship you."

Before we talk about what practices shape the *even if* life (it's one thing to declare it, another to fashion our lives by it), we'll consider one more *counter if*—the *what if*s that come from focusing on contingencies.

Any good planning involves contingency measures. As they plan for desired outcomes, wise leaders will also do the due diligence to anticipate any variables that might affect the plan. If the scenario should change, then the plan will shift to a contingency measure. Weather-dependent events have rain dates. Schools have emergency-closure communication plans. Tour groups have "planned meeting spots" in case people get separated in a crowd. Even in the thick of the COVID-19 pandemic, we faced all sorts of contingencies as to what reopening could look like.

Contingencies are a part of our daily lives, whether we're cognizant of them or not. I see this at work in my own family in how we are raising our kids. My oldest son is the responsible rule follower of our family. Yes, birth order is a real thing, and after five kids, I wholeheartedly confess that parenting has everything to do with it. We were super cautious with him. We never fed him processed food. No, as soon as he was able to consume more than purees, he gorged himself on homemade, hand-sculpted vegetarian meatballs. It was the only time we ever made homemade anything for any of our kids. We sanitized his hands at every opportunity. Baths were a part of every night's bedtime routine.

Now it's perfectly acceptable for our youngest child to be found under the dinner table, snacking on a sibling's food droppings from who knows when. My wife and I have to do collective memory exercises to recall the last time "the littles" (that's what we call our two youngest kiddos) got baths.

Besides exhibiting most of the stereotypical tendencies of a firstborn child, our oldest son is uniquely cautious and circumspect. As soon as he could talk, he would comment on my driving, expressing his concerns from the safety of his car seat. "Daddy, you're driving too fast!" was a regular part of our car conversations, interrupted by the random singing of "Twinkle, Twinkle, Little Star" or "My God Is So Big." Not too uncommon for most children.

But then his caution would rise to another level.

"Dad, do we have enough gas?"

"Are you sure that we're going the right way?"

"Are we running late?"

"What if the other person's running late?"

God forbid that the low-gas light should come on (or any other indicator light for that matter). If we hit unexpected traffic, it could lead to an emotional meltdown.

As he has gotten older, some of those cautious tendencies have remained. He is not a brash risk-taker. He's dependable and responsible. His younger brothers unaffectionately call him "the third parent." He enjoys an adventure but needs a plan for how it's going to happen. He doesn't do well with surprises or unexpected changes—an unfortunate trait to possess when you have four siblings and plans change with every illness or mood. When the day doesn't go as he expected, his disappointment becomes infectious.

It's only a matter of time before he will start creating contingency plans of his own—no longer satisfied to depend on the foresight of his parents. On his own accord, he will consider the various things that could go wrong, and he'll plan his way out of those situations, making sure that he can achieve what he desires no matter what gets in the way.

Most of you are probably thinking, *What's wrong with a plan? Isn't that just being responsible and wise? I really like your son.*

I adore him, too, and there's absolutely nothing wrong with making plans for contingencies. But left unchecked, contingency plans can subtly cause us to take the place of God. They can actually weaken our resolve to trust and worship him by strengthening our resolve to trust in our own plans and our own abilities to deliver ourselves. In many respects, contingency plans are actually the attempt to avoid the furnace in the first place.

As with the previous *counter if*s we've addressed, our *even if* declarations are a more freeing and bold way to live, delivering us from the tyranny of having to safeguard our own fates and take care of ourselves.

UNMASKING OUR CONTINGENCY PLANS

Contingency plans come from the desire to stay in control. In anticipating all the possibilities in a given situation, we try to guess what the future will be like and prepare the necessary responses. We do this by asking over and over, "*What if* . . ." Similar to fantasy regrets, *what if*s live in the imaginary world. The difference is that while *if only*s compare where I am now to where I imagine I should have been by now, *what if*s compare the future versions of my life to the other future possibilities.

The ambitious young adult at the beginning of her career or family life makes several versions of a five-year plan—the main one that guides decisions today, and the backup one in case a promotion comes earlier than expected or a child changes the picture. Some even have backup plans for their backup plans.

Hardworking, responsible adults spend hours going through the *what if*s of retirement planning and wealth management, calculating how much they're worth as stocks rise and fall.

Hopeful parents meticulously consider the *what if*s of their children's education, making sure they have access to all the extracurricular activities and growth opportunities that will keep them above a certain percentile.

Patients and their caregivers in the midst of illness have to ask the *what if*s of treatment plans. Each decision and course of action depends on the next bit of data and the body's reaction. Contingency after contingency.

*What if*s aren't limited to these huge decisions. On a daily basis, we wonder *what if* about the immediate situations we find ourselves in. *What if I fail at this project? What if they don't like me? What if people discover who I really am?*

What ifs are inevitable. It's what we do with our *what ifs* that can run counter to resolute and confident faith. Unwilling to accept the possibility of failure or outcomes we aren't prepared for, we labor over our contingency plans as we try to manage lives that are inconveniently beyond our control. And our contingency plans are never alone. They are always accompanied by anxiety and fear as we ask, "*What if* my plans don't work out?" The result is a neurotic preoccupation with our plans that grows with every anxious thought.

No one likes being anxious or afraid. So we will do whatever we can to minimize or avoid trouble. Which, in turn, feeds our anxiety. As we imagine what might happen, the threats on the horizon, we double down on our contingency plans, and the cycle repeats itself in endless rounds of *what ifs*. We have all experienced what Max Lucado described:

> Anxiety is a meteor shower of what-ifs. What if I don't close the sale? What if we don't get the bonus? What if we can't afford braces for the kids? What if my kids have crooked teeth? What if crooked teeth keep them from having friends, a career, or a spouse? What if they end up homeless and hungry, holding a cardboard sign that reads "My parents couldn't afford braces for me"?[1]

Admittedly, writing out the progression of the cycle makes it look a little silly, but in the moment, the anxiety is a very real and threatening struggle. Our imaginations run wild, and we figure out contingency plans as a response.

The strength and number of our contingency plans are based on the resources we believe we have available. The more we believe we have the ability to control our lives, the more contingency plans we'll create. The more we think we are on our own, the more we will rely on our own strength and wisdom. When we feel like things are beyond our control, we will look for ways to shore up our resources, to save ourselves from our situations.

In that way, contingency plans are a means of self-protection. As we imagine and predict the ways life could go sideways, we attempt to hedge our bets and stay in control. Life may try to sabotage our best-laid plans, but we'll outsmart it by having better plans. "Be prepared" is the rule of faith for the contingency maker. In hedging our bets, we can even rationalize it as responsibility or good planning, not realizing that all the while we are trying to exert control and, in essence, play the part of God.

Jesus spoke to our tendency to make *what if* plans in his best-known sermon. He told his disciples, "I tell you, do not be anxious about your life, what you will eat or what you will drink, nor about your body, what you will put on. Is not life more than food, and the body more than clothing?" (Matthew 6:25).

Don't overlook the fact that this admonition against worry follows Jesus's statement that no one can serve God and money (verse 24). At the heart of it, he was calling out our tendency to trust in our own abilities and resources. In no other place did Jesus call out a specific competitor for our affections.

In other words, don't be preoccupied with trying to provide for yourself. Don't give your allegiance to your own resources. This is how we plan for contingencies—we allocate our resources to ensure that what we want to happen, happens. As long as we have enough resources, we think we can handle anything that should come our way. And should we not have enough, anxiety rules.

His corrective to trusting in our contingency plans is to remember that "your heavenly Father knows [what] you need" (verse 32). He pointed us to the wise, kind, and providential character of our heavenly Father—all nuanced expressions of his goodness. He knows what we need, Jesus pointed out, and he will provide for us just as he does for the birds of the air and the flowers of the field. Here again is the first part of the *even if* life: remember the goodness of your Father.

THE BIRTH OF THE CONTINGENCY PLAN

With an idea of why we make contingency plans—a desire for self-preservation, the need to be in control—we can now unpack how we go about forming them. Contingency plans usually start in one of two ways. The first is by arming ourselves with more knowledge. The reasoning goes that the more I know about something, the more I can guarantee the success of my plans. This is the research and development phase of our contingency plans.

If you've ever faced a situation where you've felt powerless, then you've probably done the "Google deep dive." It usually unfolds like this. You come up against some diagnosis or challenge that concerns you. So you google it, summon Siri, or ask Alexa. You scan the resultant sources, then click on a link that feels legitimate. One article leads to another. Research and case studies refer to other situations that are conveniently hyperlinked, and you find yourself neck deep in all sorts of scenarios, testimonials, and recommended solutions that worked for someone somewhere.

You start trying to take notes on it all, maybe even cleverly designing some way to footnote and cross-reference, but you eventually give up. Minutes turn into hours. The more you click, the more you become overwhelmed by the amount of information you have, and your imagination runs wild, as you now have to consider more scenarios than you initially imagined. With every new scenario, you have more *what ifs* than you ever thought possible.

Run a simple medical question through a Google deep dive, and now you know the thousand things that could go wrong with a medical procedure that has a 99 percent success rate. You're even aware of the rating of the doctor you're consulting, and you've been introduced to a myriad of experimental medicines that worked. You even know what your hospital food menu options are for post-op recovery and when you should ask for the orange Creamsicle that's not on the menu.

Or if you're deep-diving into a future purchase, you read review after review of the product or service provider. You learn about all the safety ratings and manufacturer recalls. You read about others' experiences. You see how much it actually costs. Warning after warning, recommendation after recommendation provide a conflicting array of opinions. In your efforts to be an educated consumer, at the end of all the research, you feel numb in addition to being exhausted.

Welcome to the black hole of overresearch, the place where you have so much information that you experience paralysis by analysis. So many scenarios run through your head that you are afraid to take a step because you might be taking the wrong one. What starts out as a means to help you feel in control ends up controlling you as your *what ifs* take over, feeding off all the information you've gathered. Unintentionally you've constructed an iron lattice of contingencies that overwhelm you like a tax code with more possible scenarios than you needed.

Rarely does a Google deep dive lead us to more confidence or peace. And the unpleasant reality remains: we have little control over the actual outcome of whatever decision we make, no matter how much information went into the process.

I'm not discounting the place of researching, asking good questions, and learning what we can know. That's wise. But we must be aware of our hearts' tendency to pursue knowledge as a way of hedging our bets, staying in control, and ultimately trying to be god. Don't underestimate the heart's inclination to self-deification. Just like in the garden at the very first (Genesis 3:5–6), we pursue some kinds of knowledge with the goal of becoming like God. Our contingency plans become mini decrees: "Thus saith me: my will be done."

In a day and age when we have more information available than ever before, discernment and self-control are more important than ever. All our attempts to research and be more informed must be in submission to the Lord who alone knows all things. "The secret things belong to the LORD our God, but the things that are revealed belong to us and to our children forever, that we may do all the words of this law" (Deuteronomy 29:29). There are some things that God wants us to know so that we can obey and trust him. There are even more things that we cannot know.

God calls us to employ our minds to know how to live wisely and courageously. He wants us to count the cost, to consider the options, but he never renounces his right to have the final word. He reveals truth to us out of his goodness, but he also calls us to trust him with the things left secret. After all the research is done, every *what if* must surrender to the confident resolve of an *even if* faith that acknowledges that God knows what he's doing and that's enough for us.

WHITE-KNUCKLING IT

A second way we form our contingency plans is through trying to tightly control our environments. While deep-diving is an attempt to control our situations through knowledge, we can also try to control them by sheer will.

When one of my sons creates a Lego scene, he will find a place away from the foot traffic of his siblings. We then end up having self-contained pop-up Lego playlands all throughout the house. I have seen him build a Lego battlefield behind the sofa under the bay window just so that his brothers will stay away. Another son will build on the dining room table, high enough so that "the littles" can't reach it.

No one gets to touch the Legos without permission. Every placement and subsequent movement is scripted with precision. The builder knows when a piece has been moved or has been "borrowed" by a sibling builder across the family room. In ways that rival the safety and security protocols of an infectious-disease lab, the builder makes sure that nothing comes in or goes out except for authorized personnel. Everything is tightly controlled.

We do the same things in life with our contingency plans. Raise your hand if you've ever crafted a tight schedule to make sure that you can maximize every moment of the day with no interruptions. Or if you've ever micromanaged your employees or helicopter-parented your children, pressing on the smallest of details to make sure that everything is done the way you want. Let's not even talk about vacation plans.

"But I have the best interests of my children at heart," you might reason. "I want to make sure that the team does its best work." "I want us to have the best time possible with the most memorable experiences and the best return," says the militant leader of a trip whose research and plan make Tripadvisor look like an amateur operation.

Like research, there's nothing wrong with planning. However, for all the control freaks among us, how do you react when the plan is threatened? When you're faced with even the smallest possibility that something unexpected might occur, your reaction can be telling. Do you respond with flexibility and make adjustments? Or do you lean in and grip tighter in order to keep everything on its original course?

Move to the next objective on the right timeline; hit the right benchmark. Apply pressure; crack the whip if it looks like you might be off schedule or off course. This type of contingency plan reacts with swift force to stamp out even the slightest potential of interruption, whatever or whoever it may be. Do what you can to control it.

This, again, is a formula for anxiety and disappointment because life never stays within the bounds of our plans. Max Lucado explained the cycle: "That's why the most stressed-out people are control freaks. They fail at the quest they most pursue. The more they try to control the world, the more they realize they cannot. Life becomes a cycle of anxiety, failure; anxiety, failure; anxiety, failure. We can't take control, because control is not ours to take."[2]

I'm writing this section in the midst of a pandemic caused by the coronavirus. If there's ever been a time when *what ifs* rule the day, it's now. Palpable uncertainty and fear surround us. The environment is way beyond our ability to control. We don't know who might be an asymptomatic carrier. We can't trust the normal places we inhabit. That's why everything was shut down. Schools are closed. Restaurants are vacant. Even the mall, that great American institution of consumer discipleship, has closed. Governments are sifting through an endless assortment of contingency plans for reopening, all the while preparing for a second wave.

At the personal level, households are making all sorts of contingency plans as well. "Do I go out?" "Should I go back to church?" "Is it safe enough to meet?" "Should I allow my kids to have playdates?" "What will happen with schooling?" "When will I regain my sanity?" With every uncertainty, there is a series of *what ifs* to go with it and corresponding contingency plans.

The *what if* frenzy was seen most clearly at the beginning of the quarantine. At the early stages of shutdowns, we experienced a hitherto-unseen toilet paper shortage. Yes, that ever-necessary ration to survive an apocalypse, a quarantine lifeline wrapped around a cardboard cylinder. Grocery stores (even Costco!) were completely out of toilet paper and sanitizing wipes. Hand sanitizer was liquid gold; it certainly was selling for more than a barrel of oil. Well-meaning, fear-filled folks fell into panic-buying household goods "just in case." Stores had to respond with policies enforcing strict "one package per customer" rations and reminders to "buy what you need."

Have you ever considered why we stockpiled (and, in some cases, continue to do so)? I wonder whether it's our attempt to carry out our contingency plans amid the uncontrollable. Stockpiling is based on the fear of "*What if* I don't have enough?" "*What if* someone gets the last one and I'm left empty handed?" We imagine ourselves on the outside, lacking basic necessities. We hear in our heads the voices of our dependents blaming us for failing to care for their basic needs. So we buy more than we need.

Most people heading to the store aren't in a frenzy to panic-buy. But like COVID-19, all it takes is one person to start an infection. One person starts throwing one too many cases of water and mass amounts of toilet paper into a cart, and *what if*–driven anxiety fuels a rush for bread, eggs, milk, and toilet paper. Contingency plans take over common sense and even love for neighbor. One *what if* leads to another, and our shopping carts fill up almost as fast as anxiety overruns our imaginations. The logical next step is to exert our wills to control by means of our consumer power.

THE BARRIERS WE BUILD

What we do at the consumer level in a pandemic, we can also live out at the relational level. All relationships have uncertainty and the possibility of change inherent in them. The unpredictability of another person can cause so many *what if*s, and we will try to control and protect what we love. It can lead to lots of frustration (and even suffocation) if we try to keep the relationships within the confines of our wills.

In his memoir, Sheldon Vanauken described this experience in his marriage. At the beginning of their journey together, Sheldon and his wife, Davy, were determined to keep their marital commitment to each other. In addition to the practices you might expect would strengthen a marriage, they also determined to anticipate and prevent anything that might threaten it. Partly out of devotion and mostly out of fear, they built what he called "the Shining Barrier" in order to protect the purity and fidelity of their love.[3] Like a wall protecting something precious from outside forces, this barrier was their attempt to safeguard their love by controlling all influences on it.

They would not pursue individual interests—they had to share everything. "If one of us likes *anything*, there must be something to like in it—and the other one must find it. Every single thing that either of us likes. That way we shall create a thousand strands, great and small, that will link us together. Then we shall be so close that it would be impossible—unthinkable—for either of us to suppose that we could ever recreate such closeness with anyone else. And our trust in each other will not only be based on love and loyalty but on the *fact* of a thousand sharings—a thousand strands twisted into something unbreakable."[4]

Create enough bonds, they reasoned, and you would not—in fact, you *could not*—choose another person. Sheldon and Davy built what they thought was a watertight, safe connection in which they could ensure that their desires for love were always fulfilled. What looked like a beautiful means to intimacy was actually an insurance plan to guarantee, even force, fidelity. They even decided not to have children, lest the children should come between them and draw affection away from the other.

Without using the exact phrase, Sheldon's commitment to Davy was fraught with *what if*s. "*What if* our love wanes?" "*What* *if* someone else comes along?" His commitment to his wife then became a series of contingency plans (shared interests, exclusivity, mutual dependence) to ensure devotion. No one would be able to penetrate the Shining Barrier of their love, not even God.

Until he did. With most of our attempts to control life, God has a way of reminding us that we're not in control. Life happens. And through the unexpected, God's grace sneaked behind the Vanaukens' defenses, saturating their hearts and softening their resistance.

The true love of God broke through the Shining Barrier, even absorbing it, and God invited them, beginning with Davy, to a deeper love than anything their contingency plans could ever bring about. Davy surrendered to the matchless love of God in Jesus. Sheldon initially refused. The thwarting of his contingency plans, the tearing down of his barrier, felt like a threat to his need to protect love.

He saw the intervention as an invasion of his will, not an invitation to experience what he'd been longing for all along. In the midst of his stubborn refusal to let God in, he grew increasingly jealous of Davy's relationship with God. God became another variable that he must eliminate. But he couldn't. He was no match for God's beauty or appeal.

Davy fell ill, and it was through the slow tragedy of losing her that he surrendered. He realized that the love that he really wanted and needed, the love that the Shining Barrier was designed to protect, was actually to be found in the love of God. The goodness that they were longing for would be experienced only as they both experienced it in God, not just each other. God was what they both ultimately longed for.

Sheldon came to understand that their attempts to safeguard their own love were actually breaking the law of love, both to their God and to their neighbor. It wasn't their commitment to loving each other as husband and wife that was the issue. Husband and wife, by God's design, are one flesh. This is beautiful and holy. But their attempts to ensure their love by their various contingency plans blinded them to the real purpose and source of love, God himself.

Once Sheldon surrendered to the love of God, it opened up his own *even if* chapter. At the death of his dear bride, his mentor, C. S. Lewis, helped him understand the notion of a severe mercy—the means by which God spared him from the actual consequences of the Shining Barrier. Their love would have suffocated to death. Rather, as their love was replanted in the goodness and beauty of God, not even physical death could extinguish it.

"If my reasoning—my judgment—is correct, then her death in the dearness of our love . . . saved our love from perishing in one of the other ways that love could perish. Would I not rather our love go through death than hate? If her death did, in truth, have these results, it was, precisely, a severe mercy."[5] In other words, should God lead my wife home, I will receive it as a mercy, even if it should be a severe one.

What about your relationships? Have you built some Shining Barriers around your children? Your spouse? Your friends? With every good intention, could you be actually looking to control your relationships in order to get out of them what only God can give?

The *even if* declaration says that only God ultimately gives us what we desire. Only he can fulfill our desires for real love and belonging. Could God be asking you to stop trying to squeeze out of the people in your life what only he can give? Will you trust in the One who can give you what you really desire, who alone can safeguard what you're afraid could be lost?

I pray you'll believe Jesus's words afresh when it comes to your contingency plans: "Whoever seeks to preserve his life will lose it, but whoever loses his life will keep it" (Luke 17:33).

COUNTERING OUR *COUNTER IFS*

As we close this section on *counter ifs*, let me connect the dots. God said this about our hearts: "The purpose in a man's heart is like deep water" (Proverbs 20:5).

So many variables influence what we do and why. I've tried to identify just three to get you started. Don't worry about trying to get all the terms right. They're just one way of trying to diagnose what's going on in our hearts. You might have *counter ifs* that are unforeseen hybrids of all three categories we've looked at: *only ifs* + *if onlys* + *what ifs*.

Contingency plans are the means by which we carry out our conditions (*only ifs*) and how we ensure our regrets (*if onlys*) never happen again. In that way, they stand in direct opposition to an *even if* kind of life. We form contingency plans as a way of being god; instead of trusting in God's goodness, we spend our energy and attention on being as omniscient or omnipotent as we can be, with disappointing results.

As you make your *even if* declaration over your *counter ifs*, at the end of the day, it's about returning to God, reaffirming his goodness, and resolving to trust in him, not yourself, not even what you see. Instead of fretting over the future, you can begin to take hold of it, knowing that no matter how it should go, God has got you.

When you declare *even if*, you will be surprised to see that each of the *counter ifs* doesn't just go away; it gets repurposed.

- You'll declare your dependence on God. Instead of the *only if* conditions of your will being done, you will ask for God's presence as the only condition you need to trust him. "*Only if* you go with me, God."
- You'll embrace the actual journey that God has carved out for you, warts and all. Instead of the *if only* regrets you can't do

anything about, you'll experience the *if only* desire to see God be glorified. "*If only* you could be worshipped and known as the great God you are."

- You'll begin to dream the *what ifs* of potential instead of the *what ifs* of precaution. What could God do here? How could he redeem? "*What if* God could take this situation in a new direction?"

Ultimately, what I pray for you is that, instead of fearing possible outcomes (*what if*), demanding only one outcome (*only if*), or longing for imaginary outcomes (*if only*), you will say *even if* because you know that though our plans will always have holes in them and uncertainties will always abound, our Father's sovereign plan will come to fruition, and it will be better than anything we could have come up with. As the apostle Paul declared at the end of his life, "I am not ashamed, for I know whom I have believed, and I am convinced that he is able to guard until that day what has been entrusted to me" (2 Timothy 1:12).

PART 3

EVEN IF ON THE STREET

Like competitors on *American Ninja Warrior,* we've run through an obstacle course of motives in the trenches of our hearts. We've run through the gauntlet of conditions that mutate from sincere desires into demands that take us hostage; the maze of regrets that constantly pull us back in time or transport us to a fantasy life that doesn't exist; even the swamp of contingencies that mires us in a thousand possible scenarios with the false belief that we can control it all.

If you're feeling tired or you're just rejoining me after some time to reflect and think, I can't blame you. It's okay to pause. Unlike on *American Ninja Warrior,* no one is keeping time, and you don't have to beat the time trial of the person next to you. Like we said about our impostor selves, God is revealing things in your heart not because he's growing impatient but because he is for you.

For me, the truth is that any or all of these *counter if*s could be ruling my heart at any given moment, depending on what hour you ask me. It seems like the moment I lay one condition down, the illusory promise of a contingency plan beckons me. Or a regret that I thought was laid to rest is reincarnated as a condition for moving forward. There's a complexity here that will always exist. But by God's grace, we will continue to sort out these *counter if*s and take them before God.

The ongoing struggle doesn't have to keep us from living *even if* lives right now. Like building a plane in midair, you don't have to sort out everything before you take a step or make your declaration. You're already on your way. In fact, as I've tried to encourage you, declaring your *even if* can be an important step in undoing a *counter if*.

In this next section, we're going to look at some of the heart postures that will help us declare *even if* and some of the actual steps that will help reinforce our resolve to worship God. Some will be obvious, but others will be intriguing, especially as we connect some dots that maybe you didn't see before.

Don't think of this as "the practical section." We're not walking into the self-help area of a bookstore. Instead, look at these next chapters as the "let's do one more rep!" encouragement of a physical trainer. We're going to practice declaring *even if* by learning some specific exercises that will shape our motivations and bring results.

If you're ready to add an *even if* lifestyle to your *even if* declaration, read on and be ready to do something.

7

It Starts Here

The spring of 2020 was terrible. Over the course of those fourteen or so weeks, my family and I had to learn some new rhythms. In fact, the entire world had to. Simple activities that we took for granted, like eating out or going to the store, were all taken away. Music lessons, sports practices, even our church functions, all went virtual for our family. We wondered how we would ever survive.

As the weeks turned into months, we adjusted. We went through several stages as the world changed around us. First there was the "this is kinda cool" phase. We all learned to use Zoom. Sure, seeing people online or preaching to a camera felt a little odd, but over and over again, we said things like "Thank God for the technology to be able to do this." We were surprised that technology allowed us to stay connected, and we were grateful.

We learned new rhythms of washing our hands, and we were alarmed to discover just how many times we touch our faces in a given hour. We sanitized at every opportunity. We became so accustomed to wearing masks that they have become a fashion accessory as well as a hygienic way of loving our neighbors.

Then it became a grind. We entered the "this is getting old" stage. People on our virtual calls started falling into stereotypical categories. The person who was always outside during the call. The person with the barking dog or crying baby. The person who couldn't ever seem to figure out the coordination required to mute/unmute at the appropriate time. The person who decided to change his virtual background every meeting. The person who never turned her video screen on. What started out as cute idiosyncrasies morphed into major annoyances.

We began to feel the burning sensation in our hands as they cracked from washing over and over again. The long, socially distant lines outside the grocery store added so much time to simple errands. I won't even mention the plight of those who have school-age kids stuck at home.

Speaking of kids at home, that's the third stage: "God, help us." In this phase, we learned that screen fatigue is a real thing. Added to that, we grew exhausted from having all our relationships—social and work—compressed into the confines of our living quarters with permeable virtual boundaries to separate them. We wondered how on earth we'd ever go to school again, let alone a concert or sporting event. It seemed bleak as we longed for reprieve. You can watch only so many Netflix shows.

Then we were introduced to the idea of phased reopening. Essential, then nonessential, businesses started to reopen. Churches began to have limited gatherings. We could get haircuts. We could eat at these things called restaurants where our food magically appeared and the empty dishes were then whisked away. Even a vaccine appeared, first on the horizon, then just within our reach.

As we reengaged life, something unexpected happened inside us. Many of us were hesitant to venture out. In the throes of our quarantine, we longed to return to life as we knew it, but then when given the chance, many of us paused.

We didn't realize that while we were trying to survive, we were actually changing. Those new rhythms were calcifying into a way of life. Through a combination of constraint, necessity, and repetition, we formed habits that have now made it hard to go back to how we did life before.

I'm trying to paint not a bleak picture but rather an encouraging one. We've learned through 2020 that as difficult as it is to break a habit, it is possible. And not only is it possible; sometimes it is also absolutely necessary. We can change old habits not just by trying to stop some behavior or way of thinking but by forming a new pattern, a new way of living. What your emergence from COVID-19 life proves is that, with enough repetition, you can live differently. In this last section, we'll learn how.

THIS IS THE GOOD LIFE

Before we zoom in (sorry—I had to use the word) on the practices of the *even if* life, it will be helpful to understand how our actions actually shape what we live for. In his book *You Are What You Love*, the philosopher Jamie Smith reminded us that we are first of all creatures of habit, formed by our practices. That means that before we are creatures who think, we are creatures who act.

Our actions are informed by what we value, what Smith called our picture of "the good life."[1] If your picture of the good life is financial security, you'll save and spend accordingly. If it's well-rounded kids, you'll parent a certain way. If it's leaving a legacy, you'll spend your time in ways that are different from someone who wants to make a name for himself.

I haven't told you anything you didn't already know. Where Smith really helped me was by showing that not only do my actions come from my vision of the good life; they can also help shape it. In other words, while what you desire will inform how you act and what you move toward, the opposite is also true. How you act and what you move toward can also shape what you desire.

At every moment of the day, we engage in practices that promise us the good life. Smith called these "liturgies."[2] It's a fitting word because liturgies are usually thought of in the context of worship. We worship what we believe has worth, what we believe will give us happiness, purpose, and meaning.

If you don't believe me, spend some time people-watching at a mall. If you don't remember what a mall is, think of an analog, in-person Amazon. Storefront window displays are designed to entice. They promise, "Here's what your life could be." Watch the look on people's faces as they make a purchase. You'll catch the all-too-fleeting boost of self-esteem that comes with a new pair of shoes or outfit. It's the good life contained in a shopping bag. The practices reinforce the vision.

If you've ever started an exercise regimen, you'll also understand this dynamic. When you start out, you believe that working out is good for you. Maybe you have a vision of the "in shape" version of you. Yet the habits just aren't there. Then you decide to take a step. You join a gym or get a bike. Maybe you hire a trainer or enlist some support system to encourage you and keep you accountable. Your vision calls forth corresponding actions.

If you stick to the program, pounds fall off. Energy levels rise. You start hearing more compliments from people. You notice how you feel when you miss a workout. The practices begin to work the other way. Instead of flowing from your vision, they begin to shape your vision. Eventually and with enough repetition, the practices become habits that reinforce your vision, even when you momentarily lose motivation.

The same holds true for living out an *even if* faith. We've spent the first part of this book unpacking the components of the declaration itself—*confidence in the goodness of God + the resolve to worship him.* We've tried to uncover the obstacles that can stand in the way. In doing so, we've attempted to put together a picture of the *even if* kind of "good life."

But understanding something doesn't mean mastery. One of my sons is learning to play the viola. His first few lessons were all about how to hold the bow, how to tuck the instrument at the right angle beneath his chin. He learned each string's note, how to tune it, how adding pressure as he moves the bow across a string changes the intensity of the sound—all the necessary elements of playing the viola. After a month of learning these basics and about a thousand agonizing iterations of "Hot Cross Buns," he understands how the viola works, but he is not anywhere near knowing how to actually play it.

Understanding is certainly required to approach mastery, but mastery comes only as whatever understanding we possess is worked out in the rigors of real life. As the saying goes, "practice makes perfect."

To really live *even if* lives, we need the practices that, with enough repetition, can become habitual ways of living in the world. We need liturgies that not only flow from *even if* faith but also form us into *even if* people. There are so many *even if* practices we could talk about, some that are unique to your situation and what you're facing. It wouldn't be helpful to you to try to list all of them.

Rather, because our speech and actions flow from our hearts, we'll start with the basic motivations of *even if* people. These motivations form the posture from which an *even if* declaration arises.

A posture is a natural stance. You're probably hearing the nagging voice of that person who constantly reminded you, "Don't slouch! Stand up straight!" You might have responded by straightening up when you were corrected, but when that person wasn't around, you went right back to slouching.

Just as you have a physical posture, so you also have a heart posture—a stance or disposition that you default to. Some people have the heart posture of complaint. They can see only what's not right or how someone fell short. Others have the heart posture of being overly optimistic. They refuse confrontation because everything is just peachy.

Heart postures need correction just as physical ones do. As with correcting a slouch, it takes work to change your heart posture, to change the ways of thinking and living that you've become accustomed to. It takes small practices performed repeatedly to develop the new habits that define a posture. At first, the practices feel awkward, forced even. But with enough intentional repetition, what started out as unnatural can become second nature.

This is true for faith as well. If you've built a habit of giving in to your *counter ifs*, if your conditions, regrets, or contingency plans shape how you live in this world and how you relate to God, you'll need to form new *even if* habits, not just make a declaration.

START WITH THE OBVIOUS

On May 21, 1997, Fred Rogers received the Lifetime Achievement Emmy Award, along with a standing ovation. He was being recognized for his faithful, influential brand of children's programming on public television. Entire generations grew up as his neighbor. In his usual humble and gentle style, he disarmingly thanked all those who had helped him along the way. Then he did something no one was expecting.

He addressed the celebrity audience: "All of us have special ones who have loved us into being. Would you just take, along with me, ten seconds to think of the people who have helped you become who you are? Those who have cared about you and wanted what was best for you in life. Ten seconds of silence. I'll watch the time."[3]

The crowd chuckled at first but then realized he was being serious as he looked down at his watch. What followed was ten seconds of thick, silent emotion as the camera panned over well-known television personalities welling up with tears, visibly taking the steps down memory lane. A simple ten-second communal practice of gratitude changed the whole room.

Gratitude is the right and first response to God's goodness in our lives. As we remember God's goodness, we give thanks. Gratitude does more than just acknowledge God's goodness. It also acknowledges who we are and therefore has a way of giving perspective to whatever situations we find ourselves in.

"To give thanks" in the original Greek comes from the root word *charis,* which means "grace." It's prefixed by *eu,* which means "good." A eulogy or a euphemism is a good speech or phrase. When we give thanks, we acknowledge the "good grace" we have received. We didn't deserve the kind act or thought.

Be it to the server who brings us a meal or the friend who gives us a thoughtful gift, giving thanks says, "I am not self-sufficient. I am connected to—and therefore dependent on—someone or something else." To be grateful is to remember that someone is constantly taking care of me and meeting my needs.

The people I most enjoy being around are those that express gratitude for the things I take for granted. They have a way of reminding me what's important without ever having to tell me. One of my good friends, John, came to know Jesus later in life. The first time he set foot in a church, he was convinced that the building would shake and the lights would flicker. Then God saved him. John has never been the same. Everything changed—his career, his marriage, his parenting. John's life overflows with gratitude. He even has the T-shirts to prove it.

John and I have been on many hiking/fishing adventures together. We've introduced other men to the joy of fly-fishing—and also the joy of following Jesus. Our friendship has deepened as we experience the power of God both in creation and in changing lives. Every adventure, whether a fishing trip in the backcountry or a post-Bible-study time at Panera, is filled with pauses where he acknowledges, "I can't believe that I get to experience this with you. How good God is to me." To me, it's another fish or another conversation. To John, it's an encounter with a good God who gives us more than we deserve.

Grateful people have a way of putting life's situations into perspective. Their gratitude clears the dust in the room, filtering out all the airborne particles of complaint and complacency that threaten to diffuse the light of God's goodness. John hasn't gotten over his life-changing experience of being given a new start through the forgiveness of his sins. His gratitude to God oozes out of his pores. It should be no surprise to you that he is a man of *even if* faith.

GRATITUDE AND *COUNTER IF*S

Gratitude is the motivation that undergirds the *even if* declaration, because gratitude leads to worship, and worship leads to contentment. When you are grateful, you recognize the kindness and goodness of God toward you in subjective ways. You were in need and were given something that you could not and did not provide for yourself. Breath in your lungs. A timely word. Hope. Strength to endure. *Even if* your life is not what you thought it would be, your life is full of God's grace delivered in a thousand dispensations.

Gratitude is the right response to God's manifold grace. When you're in an uncomfortable and seemingly hopeless situation, gratitude can broaden the horizon of your situation by reminding you of God's countless acts of provision. You find the resolve to say *even if* as you gratefully recall the ways God has cared for you.

Gratitude also weakens the power of our conditions, regrets, and contingency plans. It weakens our conditions by reminding us of what God has already done for us, *even if* it may not have been what we wanted. Our unmet conditions are severed from the erroneous conclusion that because God didn't do what I wanted, I have nothing. Gratitude resets my vision to see that though I may not be where I expected, God has not abandoned me. I can be thankful for the ways he has sustained me and the daily provisions he has given.

Gratitude lessens the burden of our regrets by weighing them on the scales of the gospel of grace. The apostle Paul showed us how. I can imagine how many regrets Paul felt as he thought about his former life as a Pharisee. He had witnessed, even approved of, the stoning death of one of the early church's leaders, Stephen. Paul recounted how he was the chief of sinners (1 Timothy 1:15).

In his letter to the church in Rome, Paul reflected on the way in which his love for the law of God continually warred against the law of sin in his flesh. He was unable to do the good he wanted to, and the very things he didn't want to do, he did. Have you ever been there? Have you ever wrestled with an attitude, disposition, or habitual sin that you knew was contrary to God's desire? If so, then you know what Paul was feeling.

Paul expressed his frustrations: "Wretched man that I am! Who will deliver me from this body of death?" (7:24). Can you sense the longing? Can you feel his regret?

What did Paul do? He answered his regret with gratitude: "Thanks be to God through Jesus Christ our Lord!" (verse 25).

Paul's gratitude wasn't a way to avoid the regrets that he felt. It's not just a cheery, "look at the brighter side" pep talk. In the very next sentence, he summed up the situation again: "So then, I myself serve the law of God with my mind, but with my flesh I serve the law of sin" (verse 25).

Yet his gratitude prevailed over his regret. In the next verses, he concluded, "There is therefore now no condemnation for those who are in Christ Jesus. For the law of the Spirit of life has set you free in Christ Jesus from the law of sin and death" (8:1–2).

Paul expressed gratitude because of the freedom that was already his. He recognized God's gracious provision. Who would deliver Paul from this body of death? Jesus. Jesus had taken the punishment that the law of sin and death demanded, the punishment Paul deserved for all his past mistakes. Jesus died for the past failures and the current frustration. "There is therefore now no condemnation." No past can jeopardize that. A new, real future is possible.

Finally, gratitude counters the anxieties that often drive us to make our contingency plans. When the *what ifs* of life threaten to consume us, gratitude reminds us of all that God has already done. God's past faithfulness assures us of his future trustworthiness. As we remember, we are released from anxiety over the maddening array of possibilities. While not making our future courses any more certain, gratitude makes us a little more comfortable with the possibilities by reminding us of the God who has provided for us until now. He can be trusted.

Max Lucado said it another way: "The anxious heart says, 'Lord, if only I had this, that, or the other, I'd be okay.' The grateful heart says, 'Oh, look! You've *already* given me this, that, and the other. Thank you, God.'"[4] In essence, the way to live in faith is to go from *what if* to what is, and if we take the time to be deliberately grateful, we'll be reminded of just how good God has already been.

LET YOUR *EVEN IF* ARISE

Gratitude will lessen the hold of your *counter ifs*, and it will motivate your *even if* declaration. Your confidence in God's goodness grows as gratitude brings to mind specific ways in which God has been good to you. Growing confidence invites greater resolve to trust him no matter how the road ahead might unfold.

Last year, I had the chance to visit one of our church members after yet another painful surgery, this time for her spine. I'm grateful that it was before COVID-19 lockdowns made it impossible to visit nursing homes. This dear sister has endured countless surgeries for her hips, legs, and spine over her entire life.

As a young adult, she spent months laid up in bed in a full-body cast as doctors tried to correct her skeletal system. She has been in constant pain for more than forty years. If anyone has a right to be resentful for the life she's been given, it's her.

When I entered her room, she greeted me with a beautiful countenance of joy in the midst of pain, a smile superimposed on a wince. We talked about her life, her suffering, the landscape of pain and disappointment she had traversed. In recalling each leg of the journey, she would talk about the faithful presence of God, how God had been so kind and faithful to her. As she lay there, it was not the brace that was supporting her but her gratitude to God.

"I'm not saying that I want this pain, but I'm okay with it because God died for me and loves me," she concluded. She knew who she was and to whom she belonged. No amount of suffering could change that. I was in awe. I had gone there to minister to her, but she had turned the tables. I was reminded of Jack Deere's reflection in his memoir: "What was more supernatural? A healing, or a heart that still worshiped as [sickness] ravaged the body in which it beat?"[5]

Underneath that profound confession of faith was a river of

gratitude flowing from the spring of grace. No matter how hard life had been, she knew she was loved because of what God had done for her in Christ. She demonstrated to me the power of the preposition in 1 Thessalonians 5:18: "Give thanks *in* all circumstances" (emphasis added). *In,* not necessarily *for.*

She gave thanks not *for* her pain but *in* the midst of it, and her *even if* declaration humbled me: "*Even if* pain follows me all the days of my life, I will worship you because you died for me and love me through it all." Gratitude blooms as *even if.*

What impact would Mr. Rogers's exercise have on our confidence in God's goodness? Ten seconds of gratitude each day could shape our *even if* declarations. Lest we file this little exercise among the myriad of other projects in the "ten days of gratitude" category, let's add one additional dimension to our gratitude. Whatever comes to mind as you give thanks right now, go one step further. What does it say about who God is or what he has done?

So in addition to saying, "God, thanks for my circle of friends," add "because it reminds me of how you've created us for relationships." Or "because it gives me a place to experience forgiveness and be known."

Don't just practice gratitude, but practice theological gratitude. I'm reluctant to even add the adjective *theological,* because, really, isn't God ultimately the giver of everything we've received? All gratitude should be theological. But since it's all too easy to just be thankful in a generic way, we'll call it "theological gratitude"—gratitude that explicitly recognizes God as the giver and ground of every good thing. We'll practice gratitude that names not just the benefit received but also what it teaches us about who God is.

Do it every day and night. Begin the day and end the day with gratitude. Remember that, just like other practices, gratitude must be rehearsed.

And don't rush through it. My youngest toddler has developed the habit of taking over our dinner prayers, that time when we give thanks for the meal before us and the day that has just transpired. He will belt out the lines of a "thank you" song that the rest of the family is expected to repeat in a kind of antiphonal singing.

Thank you, Jesus (repeat)
For our food (repeat)
And the many blessings (repeat)
Amen (repeat)

It really is as cute as it sounds except for one part. He will sing the first line by painstakingly drawing out those three words as if they were the whole song. "THAAAAAAANNNNNK YOOOOOOOUUUUUU, JEEEEESSSSSUUUSSS!" And he expects us to do the same. The first time he did this, we almost choked trying to contain our laughter. After two weeks of this, I began to dread the beginning of this prayer. I just wanted to get to the meal already.

The liturgy of this mealtime song makes me realize that I'm too impatient with the practice of gratitude. Before I even finish expressing thanks, my heart is already moving on to the next thing. Compare my impatience with gratitude with the way I deal with the concerns and challenges that confront me. I choose to dwell on those.

What if we spent as much time giving thanks as we did reinforcing our conditions, replaying our regrets, or recalibrating our contingency plans? Would our anxiety diminish? Would we feel a more stabilizing sense of peace? I imagine that if we put some of the energy spent on our conditions, regrets, and contingency plans into giving thanks, we'd find our *even if* arising in new ways.

Start right now. Give thanks to God for one thing in your life. How has God shown his goodness to you today in real time? For those of you who are ready to level up your gratefulness aptitude, think about a situation that you are not satisfied with—maybe it's a situation that disappoints you, intimidates you, or just doesn't make sense. What can you be grateful for in that situation? What does it say about God? Go ahead. Try it now. I'll watch the time.

I CAN'T GET NO SATISFACTION

Practice theological gratitude long enough, and you'll become good friends with gratitude's timid cousin, contentment. I say "timid" because contentment is elusive in our culture. Everywhere we turn, we are bombarded by ads and marketing campaigns designed to show us how our lives are incomplete. That is, unless we buy the product the marketer is selling. Consumerism tells us to want more to the point of exhaustion. Our way of life is funded by discontentment.

Here's how it works. When we are not happy with where we are, who we are, or what we have, we feel a sense of dissatisfaction. While it might be fueled by marketing tactics, dissatisfaction in itself is unavoidable. Life often does not go the way we want. We are dissatisfied because it doesn't match up to what we dreamed or expected.

If left unchecked, the dissatisfaction grows, blinding to the good things we do have, what God has done, or who we are becoming by his grace. Dissatisfaction becomes discontentment. We begin to see life in terms of scarcity instead of the abundance of God's goodness. That's why conditions and regrets feed off discontentment. These *counter ifs* build a case for why God has failed us, calling forth as evidence all the ways what is doesn't match what we think should be.

In his brilliant book on forgiveness and generosity, Miroslav Volf described the dilemma that comes from discontentment.[6]

Namely, that no matter how much we possess or achieve, there's always more to have or become. That new product or promotion that brought us such satisfaction a hot minute ago eventually loses its luster. The latest device, even with its gazillion-megapixel camera, grows obsolete. Our crowning achievements fade into memory. For even the most successful people, the sense of incompleteness remains. The truth is, you'll never have enough likes, followers, gadgets, or goodies because your hunger will always outpace your having.

When you live with the belief that you'll be content once you have everything you want, your inner monologue will include endless iterations of this statement: "If I could just _____, then I'll be happy." Just one more thing or one more milestone, and then you'll be content. It's an exhausting way to live, going from one temporary satisfaction to another with the belief that the next one will give you what you want.

No amount of accumulation will bring true contentment, because contentment is a disposition toward, not a conclusion about, however much or little you have. Godly contentment comes not at a finish line but during the race. It springs from gratitude all along the journey. As you deliberately take account of God's goodness in your life thus far, anything else to come is like the dessert after an incredible steak dinner. You certainly could make room for it, but you're also so content that you could carry on without it. "Thank you, Jesus" leads to "Dayenu" ("It would have been enough").

Instead of being "not enough" people, we can be "more than enough" people, learning the secret of being content no matter the circumstances because God has been good to us. J. I. Packer saw contentment as the fruit of knowing God: "Those who know God have great contentment in God." They can trust him no matter what. "There is no peace like the peace of those whose minds are possessed with full assurance that they have known God, and God has known them. . . . This is the peace which Shadrach, Meshach and Abednego knew. . . . Live or die, they are content."[7]

More than any blessing he could bestow, God gives us the foundation for contentment in Jesus. In Christ are the riches of God's glory, and those riches are available right now to those who love and trust him. Paul prayed it over and over again for the churches that they might know "what are the riches of his glorious inheritance in the saints" (Ephesians 1:18) and reminded them that all their needs would be met "according to his riches in glory in Christ Jesus" (Philippians 4:19). He wanted them to remember what they possessed and that "godliness with contentment is great gain" (1 Timothy 6:6).

It goes without saying that contentment forms the backbone of *even if* resolve. We determine to trust God for whatever should come, because he has been good thus far. We are content because he is enough. Whatever God should ordain for the remainder of our lives, though it may not always be agreeable, we will accept out of gratitude for all that he has already given.

I experienced this in a major turning point of my pastoral journey. When my wife and I agreed to accept the call to leave our church community in Chicago, we were nervous. The church had loved us through our newlywed years and as we became first-time, second-time, and third-time parents. They cared for us and modeled what it looked like to raise children in the church.

In addition, our congregation directly influenced the kind of pastor I wanted to be. They sharpened me, encouraged me, and loved me so graciously. Our church life embodied an adaptation of the old adage: "It takes a church to raise a pastor." Simply put, I wanted to be the kind of pastor they deserved.

The thought of moving back to our home state of Maryland was daunting and illogical at best. There were too many good reasons to stay. My mentor was getting ready to pass the baton to

me, calling me to lead the church as its next senior pastor. We
loved our neighborhood and felt a sense of ministry and purpose
there. We had come to love the resilient refugee community
around us, and friendships were deepening.

And now God was calling us to pack it up and go back to the
land of our youth. As we considered the move, all sorts of *what ifs*
plagued us. *What if* the new church ended up being a poor fit?
What if the ministry failed? *What if* our three kids hated it? *What
if* it was all just a huge mistake? Even with those questions lingering, we decided to say yes.

Ultimately, what gave us the courage to take the step was an
even if declaration that arose from gratitude and contentment. In
discerning God's will, my wife and I spent long conversations
counting our blessings, the myriad ways in which God had formed
us, loved us, and cared for us through our church. God had been
so kind to take us from everything we knew in Maryland to a
church that became our family as we "grew up." We had no reason to distrust him, even if we had no guarantees for the next
step.

Our hearts and lives were full, and we could say like Paul, "I
have learned in whatever situation I am to be content. I know
how to be brought low, and I know how to abound. In any and
every circumstance, I have learned the secret of facing plenty and
hunger, abundance and need. I can do all things through him who
strengthens me" (Philippians 4:11–13). *Even if* the next ministry
didn't work out, *even if* we were making a big mistake, we would
follow the Lord into the next chapter.

We packed it all up and moved. It turned out that the next two
years of ministry were some of the most difficult I had ever experienced. I had many regrets, often feeling that I had made a huge
mistake. Relationally, we started over. I had to build trust and
credibility with an even larger congregation. A moral failure
rocked our staff team. We went from being homeowners and

leaders in our neighborhood to living with my in-laws. I wanted to go back to Chicago.

What enabled me to endure those hard years was the regular practice of gratitude. I started with the past. I had never envisioned ending up in Chicago in the first place, yet God had taken me as a broken would-be pastor, banished to the wilderness, and replanted me in Chicago for growth and restoration.

Then I moved to giving thanks for what I had in front of me. I had a hungry group of young adults with whom to do life. The missional opportunities in my neighborhood, while not the same, had potential. I was surrounded by family. My kids were doing well.

Slowly I became content even though my situation didn't change. I began to speak a dayenu for new challenges that came my way. I learned that contentment and dissatisfaction can coexist in an *even if* faith. You don't have to like where you are, but you can still be content that God is with you in the midst of it.

Even if where I found myself was not what I had imagined, I would still trust God. I knew that God had led me here and that he would, in his own timing, lead me out. And *even if* this stop in Maryland was to be a short one (it turned out it wasn't), I would fulfill the calling that God had placed on me, bringing to bear all the things he had taught me as a pastor in Chicago.

As best as I could, I resolved to worship God by loving his people for as long as he would have me with them. No matter how my ministry turned out, I would trust God with it because it all belonged to him anyway. He had never abandoned me, even when I had given him plenty of reason to. He wouldn't start now. Gratitude and contentment gave me the resolve not to just endure those years but to worship God through it all.

Your *even if* declaration might not involve the same decision points as mine, but it will flow from the same fount of gratitude and contentment. As your heart is shaped and softened by the good ways God has cared for you, you will find that the habits of giving thanks and being content will lead to freedom to really love and worship God no matter the circumstances.

In the next chapter, we'll imagine what that freedom could look like.

8

Permission to Speak Freely

Several years ago, God called a faithful couple from our church to serve him overseas. It wasn't a total surprise actually. They had built an effective ministry among international students and workers living in our community, and their heart to see the most unreached come to know Jesus was only growing.

As they raised support and made their plans, their journey took a major turn. They got pregnant. Their original plan was to move overseas and establish their lives and ministry before trying to raise a family, but even with this unexpected development, they pressed forward. They decided that *even if* their move involved more than they had originally planned for, they were going to obey God's call and move overseas. They trusted God's goodness to provide for all their needs, whether as a couple or as the parents of a newborn.

God was faithful. He made both their ministry and their family fruitful. Over the next six years, two more children came along. God even used their children to open many doors for building relationships with neighbors, connecting them in ways that would have been much harder as a childless couple. Their children's love for God encouraged them and challenged them to grow in faith.

Seven years into their journey, while on a holiday trip, their oldest son began to feel fatigued. They thought nothing of it, assuming he had the kind of cold that comes with being an outgoing young boy. At bedtime, a fever developed. They gave him some Tylenol, and he fell asleep. Nothing out of the ordinary. A few hours later, they awoke to him moaning in bed, and when they checked on him, he was unresponsive.

What followed was a blur as they rushed him to the local hospital. By midnight, the unimaginable had occurred. Their otherwise-healthy firstborn son, the one whose very life was a reminder of their *even if* resolve, inexplicably died of a common infection that had attacked his heart.

To add insult to injury, their hotel room was quarantined as a crime scene, mother and father under suspicion because of the mysterious nature of his death. Questions were followed by a medical exam. And after all was said and done, the medical team decreed that it was just bad luck.

Just bad luck? That's what you say when the restaurant is out of your favorite dish or you miss out on scoring tickets to a concert. A tragedy like theirs went way beyond the realm of luck. In fact, their faith in a good God compelled them to ask tougher questions. They wrestled not only with the question "Why?" but also with the question "Now what?"

We've learned and believed over the years that there's a God who is in control, who loves us and has a good plan for our lives. But where was he that dark night? Was luck determining our fate? We can't believe that; it's too hopeless. God knew what was happening, and allowed it to play out that way. Would we praise him "even if" He didn't save [our boy's] life?

The journey over the next year was a fog of grief, anger, and confusion. The pain was deep. There's an amount of uncertainty and suffering that anyone who follows God's call should expect, but this seemed well beyond the bounds of what is fair and appropriate. Coffins should never be made that small. No one prepares for this.

After a local funeral, the entire family returned to the States to bury the body of their little boy and to grieve with the faith community that had sent them out in the first place. Father and mother walked the same path but in different lanes, each processing and grieving at his or her own pace. The pain of a bereft mother and father is hard to overstate—the daily horror of waking up and realizing, *Oh no, this nightmare is reality.* Both shed many tears in the context of prayer, counseling, community, and worship. Our entire faith community was at a loss.

After a period of mourning, they continued their grief journey by returning overseas to the country where their son had passed away. More questions and uncertainty abounded: How could they go back and relive it all? How would they fare with a four-year-old and an infant while in the valley of grief? Yet they did that which they had done at the beginning of this whole crazy journey: they resolved to believe and obey *even if* they didn't understand.

Around the one-year anniversary of their little boy's passing, God met each of the parents in powerful ways. A new *even if* declaration was birthed from heaviness and pain. The *even if* you declare when you have an unexpected child coming is very different from the *even if* you whisper when you've lost that child.

They declared, "*Even if* we should have to pay a terrible cost, we will worship and obey you. You are worthy of our lives and our children's lives, and we trust you." In a letter the father shared with me, he put more context to it:

I decided years ago to follow Jesus, and even if the worst happens, I will still follow. Jesus is not worthy of our worship because he does what we want him to. Jesus is worthy because he is the eternal Word of God. In each of our own timing, we chose to believe that God is worthy of all honor and glory even though our son was torn from our lives. Oh, how we wish we could see it all made new. But until then, we won't concede to other gods. We still choose to bow down to only him.

Another year has passed, and they are still forming new iterations of their *even if* declaration. Each unexpected wave of grief seems to bring new opportunities to believe in the goodness of God and to resolve to worship him.

They have had to walk through a variety of *counter ifs*. All kinds of *if only* regrets bruise their consciences as parents. Understandably, they wonder what might have made that painful night end differently. "*If only* we had paid more attention to the fever." "*If only* we had been in our home city." "*If only* we had known what was going on."

Imagine the kinds of *what ifs* that flare up when one of their children has any sort of sickness now. Imagine the *what ifs* of living through a COVID-19 quarantine after losing your firstborn to a freak infection.

Just as their story is still being written, so is their *even if* declaration. An *even if* declaration doesn't mean immunity from ongoing struggle, nor does it mean that everything after will be clear and straightforward. It's not a one-and-done deal. Their responses haven't been perfect. Their resolve has not been immovable. Their faith has had its high and low points. This journey has not been easy, but God has shown them his goodness in the midst of it. They are not walking in the furnace of loss alone.

That's how the *even if* life is formed. As God's grace meets one disappointment, one doubt, or one fear at a time, we respond to each with confidence and resolve to worship God through small steps of obedience and devotion. With each step, confidence builds on confidence; resolve makes possible more resolve. You don't have to have it all figured out at the first glimpse of a fire.

In the previous chapter, we looked at the posture that forms the foundation of the *even if* life: gratitude and contentment not only enable us to look for God's goodness but also strengthen our resolve.

In this chapter and the next, we'll describe the freedom that comes with an *even if* life. Your declaration will allow you to live authentically, both in word and in deed. We'll begin with the freedom to "tell it like it is" and then move on to taking the next step in our journeys.

SAY WHAT IS SO

Every year, I pay my dues as a parent of young musicians by attending my kids' elementary school concerts. In the pre-COVID-19 days, way too many people with way too many recording devices would pack into the school cafeteria like industrial workers amassing for a shift change. Attending kids' concerts is every bit as much a test of endurance as it is a demonstration of parental pride. I have kept the videos of many concerts just as evidence if my kids ever question whether I love them.

On one occasion, the school orchestra was uniquely out of sync. With the painful blend of out-of-tune instruments and young children whose motor skills were still very much developing, it resembled a colony of feral cats fighting over territory.

At the peak of the cacophony, my middle son couldn't take it any longer. Faced with the noise and the fact that his rear end was going numb from sitting on the metal folding chair, he cried in his outdoor voice, "This is awful!" Immediately I hushed my son, horrified but also humbled that he had voiced what I was feeling. As I looked around to survey the damage of his honest evaluation, the listeners around us all sighed in silent agreement. *Yes, this is awful.*

Unlike my young barbarian, however, the rest of us had chosen not to speak what we were feeling in the interest of preserving our budding musicians' confidence. We are taught at a young age to preserve a measure of propriety, to uphold a standard of courtesy and respect. After all, "if you don't have something nice to say," the saying goes, "don't say anything at all." How old were you when you realized that there are some things that you just aren't supposed to say aloud?

Christians live under the unspoken but agreed-on rule that we are not to express doubts, voice complaints about God, or admit confusion. We're supposed to be outwardly positive and hopeful because, after all, that's what faith is about, and no one wants to be a downer. So we keep it all inside or at least out of the public sphere. No wonder churches are notorious for their gossip mills.

The result is that we learn to ignore or suppress what we really think or feel. When was the last time you voiced your fears, your disappointments, or your real opinions? I don't mean posting rants on social media but rather entrusting yourself to another by an in-person, deeply vulnerable disclosure of where you are and who you are.

Despite the many outlets that social media offers for self-expression, most of us live our authentic inner lives on mute. To speak aloud what is really going on in our hearts feels awkward and even inappropriate. So we treat our disappointments, fears, and confusion like Lord Voldemort in Harry Potter—that which must not be named.

And in doing so, we're never fully honest with ourselves, others, and even God. That sets us up to live in our impostor selves, the fantasy lives that we believe we're supposed to live. There's no actual growth in that life. Brian Stone described it this way: "The journey of living into your dreams is fueled by a growing capacity to tell the truth about what is actually happening in your life, what we call 'saying what is so.'"[1]

Another word for this is *confession*. You might imagine confession to be that vulnerable act of naming your sins. While it certainly includes that, confession is more broadly the act of simply saying what is true. When a number of people agree on a truth, the resulting statement of belief is called "a confession." Even the Scriptures encourage us in it—to hold fast to our confession (Hebrews 10:23).

In speaking what is true through confession, we experience authenticity. Like exhaling after you've been holding your breath for way too long, confession frees us to be who we really are without faking. Whether as a confession of your faith, a confession of wrongs you've committed, or a confession of expectations gone unfulfilled, when you speak what is so, you step into a level of intimacy and connection because you have disclosed what is true in your heart.

That's why the Scriptures invite us to confess to God. When we confess sin or disappointment or fear, it's not like we're telling God something he didn't know. God doesn't respond to our confession with shock: "What? I had no idea you were so conflicted. What's wrong with you?"

No, God invites us to be authentic. He invites us to speak what is so from our hearts. Yet in great irony, God is sometimes the last being we feel comfortable sharing our deepest thoughts and desires with. As if we will offend him or trigger some divine insecurity, we hesitate to make our feelings known to the One who knit us together, instead presenting a list of requests and intercessions. We might ask for help, and we might bring our needs before him, but we rarely say what is so, what we really want—speaking our deepest desires, fears, and concerns.

As I've been reflecting on why I am so reluctant to speak to God this way, I've been drawn to one of the most powerful questions Jesus asked: "What do you want?" I admit that I have to wrestle with hearing this question in its right tone: not as the words of an annoyed Messiah whose day has been interrupted by my presence, but as the question of a concerned Savior who came to seek and to save what was lost.

Whether a blind man desiring his sight (Luke 18:41), a mother looking out for her sons (Matthew 20:21), or said sons looking out for themselves (Mark 10:36), Jesus invited his followers to name their desires, even when those desires were selfish. When was the last time you named your desires before the Lord, when you spoke what you really want, what you are really feeling? Not just pleasantries or clichés, but candid, unfiltered requests?

If it's been a while, consider why. The way we relate to God always flows from what we believe about him. What is it that you are believing (or not believing) about the goodness of God that makes you reluctant to bring your true self before him? Do you believe that he loves you only if you have it all together? Only as long as you aren't overly high maintenance? Or do you believe that, in his goodness, God invites you to come as you are? That you can't turn him away in disdain or disgust?

A reluctance to be candid with God suggests that we do not trust that God is good enough to listen. It's a sign that we are not confident in his goodness. Refraining from saying what is so can also undermine our resolve to worship him. We will, even unknowingly, turn to something or someone else for that which only God can and desires to give. When we mute ourselves, we quiet our *even if* declarations.

PERMISSION TO SPEAK

To say what is so is a biblical practice. Let me show you an example. Along with being important songs of praise and thanksgiving, Psalms is filled with hard complaints and prayers arising from confusion. Psalmist after psalmist offered raw, earthy complaints, doubts, and cries. They stated their desires, pouring out their hearts before the Lord. They give us permission to speak what is in our hearts as well as provide a model to follow.

Psalm 88 is a good example of saying what is so. Written by the sons of Korah, it begins with a cry to God: "My soul is full of troubles, and my life draws near to Sheol" (verse 3). Things were not going well. The psalm describes a situation of dire need and isolation. Where was God? Hemmed in and afflicted, the psalmists even attributed the hardship to the wrath and assault of God.

You won't sing many songs in church that sound like Psalm 88, yet it's in the Psalter, just like Psalm 23 and other psalms of reassuring faith. The brilliance of Psalm 88 is that the medium is actually the message. The psalmists voiced their complaint and real desires to God as an act of faith. Instead of pushing those desires down or taking them somewhere else, they went to God. In the face of disappointment and hardship, they looked to the God they believed is good, *even if* they were not experiencing his goodness right then.

Mark Buchanan described it well:

> [The psalmist] prays anyhow, and in this way: according to what he knows of God, not what he sees of God. Or put it this way: his praying is anchored in God's revelation of himself in Scripture, not in his firsthand experience of God in daily life. He doesn't pray because he can taste and see that the Lord is good. He prays in spite of that, contrary to the evidence at hand. What he tastes is bitterness; what he sees is darkness.[2]

That's *even if* faith—calling out to God even when we can't see him.

We see this in other parts of Scripture too. In the book of Ruth, Naomi returned to Israel, having lost her sons and her husband. She was devastated, even telling her daughters-in-law to return to their homes and find new husbands. Naomi changed her name to Mara (which means "bitter"). She had no explanations—no optimistic, faith-filled perspective. She left full and returned empty. She was bitter in her grief. By her very name, she said what was so.

We say what is so to a God who, in his goodness, gives us the dignity of a voice, an opinion on the matter. We get to speak what we had hoped would happen. We get to address the God of all wisdom and understanding and tell him that we don't like the way things are going.

And in the very act of expressing our pain and disappointments to the God of the universe, confession can turn into profession. As we say what is so, we declare what we believe, subtly vowing that *even if* life is hard and painful, we will worship God by going to him with our complaints and our cries, not to any other would-be savior. We say along with the apostle Peter, "Lord, to whom shall we go? You have the words of eternal life, and we have believed, and have come to know, that you are the Holy One of God" (John 6:68–69).

There's actually a category in the Bible for this kind of prayer. They are called laments.* Lament is the biblical practice of saying what is so sometimes as a complaint, most often as a cry. Lament is the expression of desperate dependence when all our power and control have been exhausted, our expertise shown lacking. It's the repeated chorus of "How long, O Lord?"

---

* There are many books written on the topic of lament. A few that come to mind are *The Louder Song* by Aubrey Sampson; *Rejoicing in Lament* by J. Todd Billings; and *Lament for a Son* by Nicholas Wolterstorff.

There are more laments than praise psalms in the book of Psalms, and it makes sense when you think about it. Life is hard. If you can't cry out to God in the midst of hardship, what good is faith? The sheer number of psalms of lament tells us that God gives us permission to do so as an act of faith, saying what is so with courage and confidence that God hears us.

There's even an entire book in the Bible called Lamentations. The prophet Jeremiah looked over the destruction of Jerusalem and composed a lament—saying what was so as he grieved over the fortunes of his home and the place where God had promised to dwell with his people.

My friend Aubrey Sampson wrote about the significance of the third chapter of Lamentations in her book about lament.[3] Jeremiah's lament reached a feverish swell as he confessed, "My soul is bereft of peace; I have forgotten what happiness is; so I say, 'My endurance has perished; so has my hope from the LORD'" (verses 17–18).

Having said what was so, he made his *even if* declaration. "[Yet] this I call to mind, and therefore I have hope: The steadfast love of the LORD never ceases; his mercies never come to an end; they are new every morning; great is your faithfulness" (verses 21–23). Aubrey wrote, "Jeremiah's *yet* is found in the unchanging, steadfast love of God. Through his *yet,* Jeremiah declares, 'Even if this suffering never ends, I will always worship God.'"[4]

Jen Pollock Michel described lament this way: "The act of complaining to God is not primarily about venting our emotions, not primarily about building endurance, not primarily about clawing our way back to happiness. Lament isn't the road back to normal. It's the road back to faith."[5]

So here's your permission to speak what is so. Put words to your feelings of disappointment, confusion, or anger. You could begin with your *counter ifs*. Name your unmet conditions and lay them down; give voice to the expectations that rule you. Confess your regrets to God, the ones swallowing up your memories in an infinite loop of *if only* scenarios. Call out the neurotic nature of your *what if* contingency plans.

You're not saying that what you're feeling is righteous or even justified. Your feelings are not coming into existence by your naming them. They're not becoming truer because you're finally talking about them aloud. In fact, as you name them and take them to God, you're actually relinquishing their power over you because you're resolving to worship God even with what is going on in your life and heart. *Even if* . . .

You don't have to hide your frustration, sadness, or disappointment any longer. You don't have to reinterpret your situation. You don't need to spin the facts so that your disappointments have explanations and the pain is somehow minimized.

The real power of worshipping God when all is not well is the realization that he can handle your brokenness. With each confession, you will find that God has grace for you and he does not give it in vague generalities, just like he doesn't forgive hypothetical sin. Rather, he meets you in the details of your story. He allays real fears and comforts actual sorrows. His help comes in real time as the nonfiction story that is your life unfolds. And through encountering God's grace as you name your desires and needs, you will experience the freedom to worship him in authenticity.

Risk-Takers, Daredevils, and Other People Who Make Me Nervous

Standing atop the staircase, I couldn't believe my eyes. I nervously leaned over the railing, looking down into a ravine that seemed very much out of place. This deep valley seemed to come out of nowhere. At the bottom of it lay the outline of several ancient swimming pools, identified only by the remains of stone walls poking through the overgrown grass. I couldn't believe that I was looking at the archaic remains of the pools of Bethesda, the place where Jesus healed an invalid (John 5:2–9).

I also couldn't believe how high I was, perched forty feet above the ground where Jesus had walked in his day. Until that point, I didn't realize that for the four days I had been walking through the Old City of Jerusalem, the ground my feet trod was way above the actual Jerusalem of Jesus's day.

Like the layers of a cake, modern-day Jerusalem sits atop layers and layers of rubble, each from a different era of conquest. Buildings were built on top of whatever had just been destroyed, and when those buildings were destroyed, the next settler would come in and build on top of that. Looking down to where the pools used to be, I grasped Jerusalem's violent history.

In fact, Jerusalem is just the focal point of hostility that has always characterized the land of Israel. This small strip of land connects Africa to Asia and Europe. Whoever controls this passageway controls important trade and military routes. At one point or another, nearly every major empire fought for and occupied some part of this land.

I found it troubling that, in the mysterious plan of God, he chose Abraham and promised that Abraham's descendants would inherit this land (Genesis 12:7). Through them, God would bless all the peoples of the earth. The rest is history—a history filled with hardships, as the security of the land was under constant threat from Philistines, Assyrians, Egyptians, Babylonians, Persians, Greeks, Romans, and so on, even continuing into this very day.

Why did God promise to settle his people in the most contested piece of land in all of human history? Why not settle them someplace safer? Montana is beautiful with its wide-open sky. I hear the French Riviera is nice. Korea would have been a great choice. A peninsula edged by mountains would have kept the people of God hidden and secure. Hawaii, Southeast Asia, the Pacific Northwest—I could think of hundreds of beautiful and more secure places to establish a people.

It's as if God doesn't value safety the way we do. He deliberately put his people in the way of the major world powers with the promise to be their God through it all. No matter what enemy might come, God promised to provide for and protect them as long as they remained in covenant with him. However, he never removed them from the danger surrounding them.

We can learn something about who God is. We must not confuse safety and protection. God gives us the latter without promising the former. As my wife and I raise our children, we've experienced the difference. To the best of our ability, we want to protect them from harm, those forces of ill will and evil intent on destroying them. We instruct them on the evils of racism: how they might experience it and what to do when they see it. We warn them over and over about the dark allure of the internet. We are vigilant about where they go and with whom. These are the realities of living in a broken and sinful world.

This is different from guaranteeing their safety, though. Not only can we not ensure their safety; we don't necessarily want to. Our role is not to provide a bubble that will keep them immune from the hardships and brokenness of the world. While we will do our best to protect them as they encounter difficulty, we will not remove them from it. Instead, we want to equip them with the wisdom and courage required to be a blessing to the world. The goal of protection is to eliminate harm. The goal of safety is to eliminate risk.

God is a protector. The Scriptures call him a refuge (Psalm 46:1) and a strong tower (Proverbs 18:10). The old hymn declares that he is a mighty fortress.[1] But just like his goodness doesn't mean he is docile, so his protection doesn't mean that he removes all possibility of trouble. To follow God is to accept risk.

A characteristic of every *even if* life, no matter how unique the events that form it, is that confidence in God's goodness and the resolve to worship him produce a willingness to take risks. Just like the *even if* declaration frees us to speak what is so, it also gives us freedom to take steps of obedience where the outcome is not guaranteed.

Even if people understand that success and safety aren't necessarily the indicators of a blessed life. They believe that God has been—and will continue to be—good to them. Because they resolve to worship God no matter what comes, they attempt great things for God, in obedience to God, trusting that he will protect them along the way. Are you ready to join their ranks?

RISK IS ALL AROUND

Different people have different thresholds of risk tolerance. Living through a pandemic has helped me see the spectrum. I have some friends who wanted to get together at the first opportunity. While not being reckless about it, they were willing to take a risk for the sake of connection and community. Others wanted to wait at least until phase 2 or 3. Some wore their masks even in the car. Some were the first ones to reserve a table at their favorite restaurant.

Perhaps you have friends who don't really need a plan until something goes wrong, and even then, they roll with it, making up the plan as they go. "We'll figure it out" is their life slogan, and they live it pretty faithfully. At first glance, their spontaneity and flexibility seem outlandish. Yet if you're candid, they live with a freedom that you secretly admire. They challenge you to step out in ways that you would never imagine.

Over the years, I've come to realize that I have a higher risk tolerance than most. I don't need every bit of data to make a decision. I don't need every detail of a plan worked out. I'm okay with uncertainty and put a premium on flexibility. Because of my higher threshold for risk, I've had to learn how to lead and care for brothers and sisters who have lower ones. I say this because I don't want to sound dismissive if you struggle with taking risks. I do, however, want to encourage you as to how your *even if* declaration could free you to take one.

While I'm not advocating for a blind, "leap before you look" kind of faith, the reality is that we'll never have all the details we may need to take the next step. And no matter how much data or faith we do end up with, we'll never be able to guarantee success.

John Piper defined *risk* as "an action that exposes you to the possibility of loss or injury."[2] I'd add to that definition the possibility of failure or disappointment. Some risks involve physical consequences, while other risks can be emotional, social, or professional. If you stop to think about it, risks are everywhere.

You take a risk when you send your children to school. You take a risk when you get into a car. You risk when you share what you are feeling, an idea you have, or what you are going through. You even risk when you purchase something over the internet or order food at a restaurant.

My children are always taking risks and even elevating them beyond their mother's comfort level. It's not enough for them to just walk along a railing. They feel the duty to climb on the top rail and balance on it. They see a yellow caution cone indicating a wet floor and immediately feel compelled to run across it to see how far they can get before wiping out. They make risk a way of life.

Living through their senseless risks reminds me that not all risks are created equal. There's a difference between risking your professional reputation by speaking out about what is unjust versus risking your professional reputation by posting foolish antics on your social media. Some risks are right and some risks are morally wrong.

Karen Swallow Prior differentiated them by the end (the telos) they have in view: "Taking a risk isn't virtuous if done merely out of inclination without intending some good."[3] A virtuous risk is calculated, not spontaneous. It involves measuring the good intended and then deciding to put something on the line, to be exposed to the possibility of failure or loss, because the objective is worthy.

Many biblical heroes took a risk to obey God.* One compelling example is Queen Esther. During the period of exile, she risked her life to save her own people from the wicked plans of Haman.

---

* John Piper summarized some stories from the Old Testament in *Risk Is Right: Better to Lose Your Life Than to Waste It* (Wheaton, IL: Crossway, 2013), 23–26.

Haman convinced the king of Persia that the Jewish exiles living in his realm were a threat to national security, so the king signed a decree to exterminate the Jews, not knowing that his own queen was Jewish.

Upon learning of the plan, her cousin Mordecai exhorted her to use her position to try to influence the king of Persia to repeal his decree. But Persian customs forbade anyone from approaching the king without being invited first. For Esther to approach him was to risk her very life.

Esther measured the good of saving her people, entrusted herself to God, and took a risk. Because we know how the story turns out, it's easy to overlook the real possibility of failure. The king could have turned her away or worse. In fact, the story of Esther begins with the former queen, Vashti, disobeying the king and being banished. A similar outcome was very possible.

Yet Esther put it all on the line. It was not a reckless move but a courageous one. She made a plan. Esther told Mordecai, "Go, gather all the Jews to be found in Susa, and hold a fast on my behalf, and do not eat or drink for three days, night or day. I and my young women will also fast as you do. Then I will go to the king, though it is against the law, and if I perish, I perish" (Esther 4:16). Did you catch that? Without using the actual words, Esther made an *even if* declaration: "*Even if* I should perish, I will trust the Lord and do what must be done." Her risky faith saved her people.

Do you remember the major risks you have taken, whether you intentionally sought them out or not? I'm sure you recall the people involved, the situation, even your churning stomach and second-guessing at the moment of decision. At the very least, you can probably remember when someone took a risk for or on you.

The risks we take—or choose not to take—have a way of becoming defining moments in our lives. In their book on defining moments, Chip and Dan Heath talked about the importance of risk-taking.[4] They shared several stories to make the point that, without some form of risk-taking, it's impossible to grow. "Get out there! Try something different! Turn over a new leaf! Take a risk! In general, this seems like sound advice, especially for people who feel stuck."[5]

But they went on to caution, "The advice often seems to carry a whispered promise of success. Take a risk and you'll succeed! . . . That's not quite right. A risk is a risk. . . . If risks always paid off, they wouldn't be risks."[6]

In our day of optimistic "you can change the world!" motivational talks, we need to hear this. With every risk, we must accept the real possibility of failure. In fact, pay attention to history, and you'll find that there are far more stories of risks that didn't go well than there are of radical successes.

Too often I dismiss the possibility of failure as if trust in God guaranteed the outcome. *If God's in it,* I reassure myself, *then of course it's going to succeed.* I inadvertently subscribe to a triumphal faith that has no categories for failure outside my own sinful actions. If I know I've sinned, then I can accept failure. But if I've sincerely attempted something in Jesus's name and it fails with no identifiable sin that I can point to, I'm left bewildered and disappointed.

It doesn't take long to figure out that failure and loss are expected parts of what it means to live—and to follow God—in this broken world. You will fail. More times than you care to recall.

That's uncomfortable, I know. It's why we usually encourage people to take risks by helping them imagine all the benefits that will come if they succeed. "Think of all the people it will help." "You'll grow in incredible ways." Most of these encouragements are predicated on the need for success, which might be the biggest obstacle to taking risks in the first place.

THE PRESSURE TO SUCCEED

My family loves Pixar movies. The collection of award-winning, culture-shaping, and paraphernalia-producing movies has redefined what we expect of animated pictures. Even more, the rich stories have a way of touching both adults and children. What many enthusiastic fans don't realize is how much work goes into the development of the story itself, even before production actually begins.

In his book, *Creativity, Inc.*, the former president of Pixar and Disney Animation Studios, Ed Catmull, gave a behind-the-scenes look at how several of the studio's most iconic movies were made and the challenges they faced along the way.[7] One challenge had to do with their success.

Each box office hit in the Pixar portfolio brought an increased pressure for the next one not to fail. No one wanted to be part of the first Pixar flop. Catmull noticed that a paralyzing anxiety accompanied their pursuit of perfection. Their determination to avoid disappointment was causing them to shy away from risk, a necessary ingredient for creative pursuits. The culture of success caused people to stop sharing their ideas and perspectives. Fear of failure threatened their creative processes.

So Catmull proposed a new ethos for their creative work—be wrong as fast as you can. Try new ideas, learn from the failure, and move forward. In other words, take a risk. Catmull's advice: "I should caution that if you seek to plot out all your moves before you make them—if you put your faith in slow, deliberative planning in the hopes it will spare you failure down the line—well, you're deluding yourself."[8] No amount of planning could guarantee success. They needed to embrace the risk of failure for the sake of creating something beautiful.

At the personal level, the pressure to succeed can have a similar effect, especially when identity is based on achievement. Approval comes when you succeed, and the resultant acceptance says that you matter, that you are worthy. Who you are is determined by what you do and how well you do it.*

That's why we will often look for acceptance through the affirmation of those whose judgments we deem important. Parents, coaches, friends, employers, pastors, a spouse—people whose thumbs-up can make our day or whose disapproving look can empty our sense of self-worth.

To live this way is absolutely exhausting because our acceptance lasts only as long as people remember our achievements. So if we are going to be loved, we have to keep achieving. Failure is not an option because our very identities are at stake.

For most of my life, I felt this pressure to succeed in living up to my potential. As I was growing up, various sincere and well-meaning people would tell me, "God is going to use you in a powerful way." They would offer encouragements like "God has gifted you, and you're going to be a blessing to so many." Without really knowing me, they made these pronouncements based on the early fruit of my labors or abilities.

Each encouragement was like a brick of expectation placed ever so delicately on my young shoulders, a sophisticated architectural monument to my potential. I began to believe that God himself had such expectations for my life. I assumed that God, too, would be gravely disappointed if I didn't fulfill my potential. Unintentionally, I denied the very gospel that qualified me for his service in the first place. I began to believe that it was not by grace I had been saved but by potential "upside." I believed that my life would be evaluated on the basis of how well I lived up to the hype.

Talk about pressure. I lived in a drivenness to succeed and a

* Frank Lake did incredible work on this propensity of people's hearts. He called it "the dynamic cycle."

paranoia of failure. *What if* I, like many first-round draft picks in professional sports, never panned out? *What if* I didn't earn my spot on God's kingdom squad? Since my identity was based on fulfilling my potential, I did everything in my power to see that potential realized, including eliminating risk. If a situation in my life approached even the possibility of failure, I would quickly assess whether I could turn it around, and if I sensed I couldn't, I would separate myself from the project, program, even person, as quickly as I could. It led to a miserable life of abandoning people when the going got tough. I was adept at managing my portfolio so that on the surface my life looked successful.

I've seen the need for success have similar results in the lives of those around me. My friend James, with his aptitude for theological reflection, was such a blessing to many around him. Yet his life was characterized by a failure to launch. He couldn't hold a steady job. He hadn't finished his college studies, and he had no real plans to get back into them. "One day . . ." was his life slogan. Our relationship frustrated me because he had so much potential but seemingly no desire to grow.

Through many honest, late-night conversations, I came to realize the root of his paralysis. He had grown up in a household where sarcasm and hypercritical attitudes characterized day-to-day life. He was constantly compared with his siblings. During just about every dinner-table conversation, he was reminded, "You'll never amount to anything." Cynical belittlement was served as a cold side dish with every meal.

More than anything, James desperately wanted to prove his family's prophecy wrong. Tragically, the way he went about it actually fulfilled the prophecy. The need to make something of his life was so strong that he was desperately afraid of failure. So he chose the safest route. He chose to do nothing at all.

In a divine and sobering moment I will never forget, he made a regret-filled and fearful confession: "I haven't done anything with my life because as long as I never attempt anything, I'll never fail." His lack of ambition was actually a fear of failure in disguise.

Is that the life that God wants for you? Is that even the life you want for you? A life so dependent on success that you never attempt anything at all? A life controlled by a fear of failure? That's what we choose when we avoid risks at all costs. The only realistic way to guarantee success is to attempt nothing at all, and that is a bigger tragedy than any failure you might experience.

While the short-term consequences of not taking a risk might seem beneficial, the long-term effects are debilitating. As was true for James, we can be safe but also totally stuck. In our attempts to manage our successes and failures, we can deny the very calling of God on our lives. While the thought of taking a risk might scare us, the thought of not taking one should as well.

That's because God calls us to more than safe lives. He calls us to take steps of obedience. In that sense, his calls always involve some sort of risk. We will never fully know what the outcome of those steps will be. Mark Batterson said it best: "Quit living as if the purpose of life is to arrive safely at death. . . . Set God-sized goals. Pursue God-given passions. Go after a dream that is destined to fail without divine intervention. . . . Dare to fail."[9]

Isn't that, after all, what the *even if* life is all about? Come success or failure, fertile valley or raging fire, I will worship you. I will trust in your goodness to me, a goodness that promises unfailing protection even in unsafe places.

FREE TO FAIL

The *even if* declaration can set us free from the enormous pressure to be significant or successful before we even lift a finger or take a step. We are reminded of really good news: that our identities are based not on what we amount to but on who God has declared we are in Christ. We are his beloved, and he will ensure that we reach whatever potential he deems good. "He who began a good work in you will bring it to completion at the day of Jesus Christ" (Philippians 1:6).

That means that, instead of working for a future secured by our successes, we turn to the One who secured our ultimate futures despite our failures. Freedom comes when we declare, in humble and grateful confession, that *even if* our lives reach none of the potential that people see, we will still worship the God who gave us life in the first place. We will declare that God didn't call us from death to life because of the great return we could give him, because we had some sort of "kingdom upside." He saved us because of his great love for us.

And when we begin to live in this truth, an unexpected thing happens. Instead of being buried under the burden of people's expectations, we can receive them as a reminder of our good God whose only expectation of us is to trust him. Instead of fearful passivity, we actually begin to attempt hard work in the world because we have nothing to lose. Succeed or fail—we are the beloved of God.

To work with all your heart—but not as if your life depended on it—is true freedom. That's the path to truly making something of the world. That's the formula for risky innovation and thinking outside the box. Because your identity is not at stake in the success or failure of a plan, you can experience the joys of seeing God's continuous provision, even when it happens to come through failure or hardship.

An *even if* life embraces risk by accepting the possibility of failure and still choosing to act. Regardless of how a situation turns out, we are resolved to worship God in it and through it, not necessarily because of it. Because we know that God is for us, we are not afraid of failure. We see it as the opportunity to know God and experience his goodness. Justin Earley described what failure can do: "Failure is not the enemy of formation; it is the liturgy of formation. How we deal with failure says volumes about who we *really* believe we are. Who we *really* believe God is. When we trip on failure, do we fall into ourselves? Or do we fall into grace?"[10]

In case you're raring to get out there and put it all on the line, embracing failure by running headfirst into it, let me remind you that the *even if* life is not an excuse for reckless behavior. *Even if* obedience comes from faith in a good God who is worthy of our lives. It is not irresponsibility excused by a fatalistic, que será, será hall pass. On the contrary, the risks you will take as a result of your *even if* declaration are calculated.

They will be the fruit of maturing, not foolish, faith. Philip Yancey described this kind of faith:

> Without an element of risk, there is no faith. . . . Faith becomes a kind of intellectual puzzle, which is never biblical faith. Faith means striking out, with no clear end in sight and perhaps even no clear view of the next step. It means following, trusting, holding out a hand to an invisible Guide. . . . Faith is reason gone courageous—not the opposite of reason, to be sure, but something more than reason and never satisfied by reason alone. A step always remains beyond the range of light.[11]

Yancey reminded us that there is always a path beyond what we can see, a little more road beyond the horizon. I know it's scary. Yes, the timing is probably not good. It never will be. Someone else could theoretically do it. But even with all the logical reasons to say no, don't sit this one out. Each risk carries with it the potential for a defining moment in your unique story, a defining moment that will make up a part of your unique *even if* declaration.

Because he is good we can believe that God can do great work through our risks: character he wants to develop in us and good in the world he wants to do through us. He is worthy of our best efforts to glorify him, and *even if* the outcome isn't what we set out for, we will worship him nonetheless.

Besides, what would life be like if you didn't take the risk? If you hedged your bets? Played it safe? Protected yourself so that no failure could ever be linked to you? You might guard yourself from hurt, but you'll also keep yourself from help. You'll miss out on what God could have done, and in so doing, you'll end up confessing like one of Screwtape's subjects in C. S. Lewis's *Screwtape Letters:* "I now see that I spent most of my life in doing *neither* what I ought *nor* what I liked."[12]

YOUR TURN

I could end this chapter with a story of someone who took a risk and show how it turned out for that person's good and for God's glory. But that would be a counterproductive disservice to you. Someone else's risk can't be the reason for yours.

Besides, there's no common currency for comparing one risk to another. Something that is a risk for me might be part of your normal living.

I was taught a long time ago that the way to discern a worthy vision for life is by answering this question: "What would you attempt if you knew you couldn't fail?" The purpose of the question is to point me to some grand cause or greater purpose that animates me or stirs passion.

While it's a helpful question, I don't think it goes far enough. I think the real question needs to be "What would you attempt *even if* you knew you would fail?" In other words, what is so important, so worthy, that you must give it a shot *even if* success is not guaranteed? That's the real definition of passion—not what excites you but what you're willing to suffer for.

With that in mind, what are you passionate about? Is there a risk that God is calling you to take? One that will make you say *even if*?

It doesn't have to be grandiose or become a viral hit. Maybe it's the risk of just getting back up again after life knocks you down. The safe choice would be to stay on the mat, but you know God wants you to get back up. As the horse says to the boy in Charlie Mackesy's fable, "Sometimes just getting up and carrying on is brave and magnificent."[13]

Maybe it's the risk of choosing to love again or opening yourself up to authentic and vital relationships. You still have battle scars, open wounds even, but you're going to try again. For sure, people can be the biggest risks we take.

Perhaps it's the risk of just showing up in Jesus's name, attempting something that will put his goodness on display. God has put a holy discontent in you about a situation that needs to change. Fostering or adopting a child. Starting a new career. Fighting racial injustice. Serving someone. Leading a Bible study. Inviting a neighbor over for coffee. Pursuing reconciliation.

All of us have ideas, latent dreams of doing something with our lives. I say that with certainty because I know that God has put them in you for his glory. Yet many of us end up putting those dreams on the shelf. They were too scary to think about. We felt inadequate. Maybe even unworthy. It's time to dust them off by stepping into the freedom that God desires for us. Name them; then believe afresh that it's time to take a risk. You might not be sure where to begin, but your confidence in God's goodness and your resolve to worship him won't let you make excuses anymore.

As God continues to write the *even if* story of your life, remember that the difference your life makes in this world will not come from the great successes you achieve. It will come from the faith-filled risks you took and the tangible next steps you believed God for, even in the midst of failure or loss.

In our last chapter, I want to give you some final *even if* encouragement to do exactly that—to take the next step.

10

Take a Step (but Not by Yourself)

The first time I set out on a multiday backpacking trip, I had no idea what I was doing or what was to come. Some college buddies and I had finished an intense discipleship journey over the school year, and our mentoring pastor invited us to celebrate it with a five-day trip into the wilderness of Mount Rainier in Washington.

I had grown up camping and always had a love for the outdoors, so I thought, *Why not?* I enthusiastically rented gear from REI, read up on the dos and don'ts, and joined my four brothers-in-arms as we set out for the great outdoors.

We got pummeled. None of us was ready for the physical rigors of a forty-mile hike over mountain passes. My rental backpack pulverized my back and hips to an almost-paralyzed state of soreness. No one told me to adjust it to fit my non-six-foot frame. On certain sections, it felt like we were a drive-through buffet for the clouds of mosquitoes that welcomed us to their domain.

The landscape was as up and down as our emotions. We had to hack our way through lush, overgrown blueberry fields as well as traverse snowpacks where one wrong step would cause our feet to plunge through the melting midsummer snow. At some points we were arm in arm, praising God for the common experience, while at others we were barely on speaking terms.

All of that was a stroll compared with the last day of our hike. We had a five-and-a-half-mile uphill climb over the final mountain pass. Bodies fatigued and emotions at the point of total collapse, we trudged through more overgrown bushes (of course, they were thornbushes this time) before we started our last ascent. As a sinister parting gift from the mountain, a dense cloud layer descended on us. After a series of intense uphill switchbacks, it was as if someone had thought, *Why not chill these weary travelers in their sweat-soaked clothes?*

I couldn't see the path in front of me partly because of the dense cloud cover and partly because my body was shivering so badly that my eyes couldn't focus. I really thought we were going to die on that mountainside. I didn't have the emotional or physical energy to finish the climb.

At the breaking point, with several of our party physically injured, we regrouped to finish the hike together. Our plan was simple as we encouraged one another, "Just take the next step. Don't look up at how far we still have to go. Keep your eyes on the path beneath you, and put one foot in front of the other."

"Take the next step." That simple encouragement not only has led me to countless backpacking adventures since but also has become a principle for life. I believe it is the most important encouragement I can give you for living an *even if* life. Taking the next step puts confidence and resolve into action. It's the way we go from considering risk to taking one. It's the way an *even if* faith gets lived out in the landscape of real life.

Your journey is going to lead you through lush places. It will also have some hard climbs and tricky descents. It's easy to get overwhelmed by wondering where it all leads, how it will turn out. Admittedly, the larger story is intimidating. The good news is that you don't have to have it all figured out in order to take the next step. Henri Nouwen encourages us, "You can't see the whole path ahead, but there is usually enough light to take the next step."[1] That's all God calls us to.

RUN TO THE BEND

My friend Jason is one of the best leadership coaches I know. One way he encourages leaders to move forward is through the illustration of running. In order to develop a running lifestyle, you have to take a step (both literally and figuratively). Buy a pair of running shoes. For the next day or week, put them on. Keep putting the shoes on even if you don't run in them just yet. When you're ready, take the next step of running.

How far do you run at first? Forget your visions of longdistance running for now. Just run to the first bend you come to. Run to the bend and back. Don't worry about what's around the bend. Don't worry about how fast you need to run. Just run to the bend. Then, the next day, run around that bend to the next bend and back. Repeat. You need to run only as far as you can see.

I used to be so afraid of where life's path would lead and how I would manage the more difficult terrain of the journey. *What if* I didn't have what it takes? *What if* I gave up? *What if* I ended up alone? *What if* I failed? My contingency plans would take over, and I'd be paralyzed. Then I'd start to make conditions under which, if God would do his part, I would set out. My imagination would run way past the bend, even before I put on my shoes.

The American mythologist Joseph Campbell observed the problem with having to have your whole path figured out before you start: "If you can see your path laid out in front of you step by step, you know it's not your path. Your own path you make with every step you take. That's why it's your path."[2] You chart your path, your faith journey, by the actual steps you take, not the ones plotted out before you.

Here's how it could work. Think about a broken relationship in your life that you know needs to be reconciled. The thought of rehashing all the hurt and navigating the various emotions and defensive maneuvering is nauseating to you. You know that there's so much history to work through. You're not even sure whether working through it will really resolve anything. Is it even worth it? What if you do all that work and then something else comes up? That's where most people give up or put it off.

What's the first bend to run to? Even the fact that you're now thinking about reconciling is an important step. Now that you've taken it, what's the next one? Will you commit to praying for that person? Not even for the opportunity to reconcile, but just for his well-being? If that's too much, perhaps begin by just speaking her name in prayer. Each step will lead to another one. You don't have to calculate what the next one will be. God will show you. You can trust him.

And no matter what comes after the next step, *even if* it's not what you expected or *even if* it's what you feared, you've resolved to worship God no matter what. You'll remember that, in his goodness, he has not failed you. You'll trust him for the courage and wisdom to take the next step and the next. That's how marathons are run and mountains get climbed: by just taking the next step enough times.

There's also the promise of what the next step could bring. A small step could bring a change in perspective. By taking a step, you're tweaking your present circumstances. That means you're opening yourself up to new possibilities, a bit more clarity about the twists and turns that you previously feared. The next step could help you see or feel things that you didn't see or feel before, and that might be just what you needed to see a breakthrough, a new path forward.

At the very least, because you've decided to step out with an *even if* faith, you will experience the presence of God no matter what comes. He promises his presence in the fire. You will have the opportunity for new experiences of provision and grace, experiences that you wouldn't have where you are right now. That alone makes the next step worth it.

An old poem by an anonymous writer but popularized by Elisabeth Elliot beckons us:

> And on through the doors the quiet words ring
> Like a low inspiration: "DO THE NEXT THING."
>
> Many a questioning, many a fear,
> Many a doubt, hath its quieting here.
> Moment by moment, let down from Heaven,
> Time, opportunity, and guidance are given.
> Fear not tomorrows, child of the King,
> Trust them with Jesus, *do the next thing*.
>
> Do it immediately, do it with prayer;
> Do it reliantly, casting all care;
> Do it with reverence, tracing His hand
> Who placed it before thee with earnest command.
> Stayed on Omnipotence, safe 'neath His wing,
> Leave all results, *do the next thing*.
>
> Looking for Jesus, ever serener,
> Working or suffering, be thy demeanor;
> In His dear presence, the rest of His calm,
> The light of His countenance be thy psalm,
> Strong in His faithfulness, praise and sing.
> Then, as He beckons thee, *do the next thing*.[3]

When you decide to take the next step or do the next thing, you will find that you're never alone in it. In fact, as you take risks to live out your *even if* faith with confidence and resolve, undergirded by gratitude and contentment, you will join the ranks of *even if* heroes, both from of old and today.

WELCOME TO THE FAMILY

Have you ever had the experience of talking to someone about a certain type of car, then seeing that car everywhere you go? It can also happen with a topic of conversation. After you talk about a certain subject, suddenly it seems like it's dominating all the airwaves around you.

Psychologists call it the Baader-Meinhof phenomenon, or frequency illusion. Once your brain gets interested in something, you notice it more. What once went under your radar now appears everywhere because your interest has been piqued. It's always been there. You're just now more aware of it. Now that you've begun to make your *even if* declaration, you'll see *even if* witnesses everywhere in the pages of Scripture even when the phrase doesn't appear. No matter how daunting your path might seem, you are not alone.

I've always been fascinated with Hebrews 11, what many teachers and scholars dub "the Hall of Faith." In encouraging us to hold fast to our confession of Jesus, the writer gave example after example of how various heroes lived by faith. They were "the people of old [who] received their commendation" (verse 2).

The list includes people we might expect: Noah, Abraham, Isaac, Jacob, Joseph, and Moses. There are also people we're surprised to see: Abel, Enoch, Sarah, Rahab the prostitute, even Gideon, Barak, Samson, Jephthah, Samuel, and the prophets. Not to take anything away from them, but Enoch or any of the judges for that matter are not usually considered exemplars of faith. Yet there they are right alongside Abraham and Moses.

I wonder how one made the list. What is it about their faith that made them worthy of mention? In pro sports, an athlete is inducted into a Hall of Fame based on a résumé of extraordinary achievements: championships, MVP awards, record-setting performances, or even the extraordinary length of his or her career. What criteria does the Bible use for its own heroes?

At the end of chapter 11, the writer cataloged the ways that these heroes lived out their faith. Some demonstrated great power, were mighty in war, and accomplished great feats. Others made the list by suffering in extraordinary ways. Some were killed. Some were homeless.

These people are inspiring for their heroic, enduring, and noble examples of faith. But that's not what got them into the hall. That's not the common characteristic. The qualifier is found in the last lines of the chapter: "All these, though commended through their faith, did not receive what was promised, since God had provided something better for us, that apart from us they should not be made perfect" (verses 39–40).

Did you catch that? They did not receive what was promised. As in, they were disappointed. God's promises went unfulfilled in their lifetimes. In other words, they had to live out an *even if* faith.

We see this qualification earlier in verse 13: "These all died in faith, not having received the things promised, but having seen them and greeted them from afar, and having acknowledged that they were strangers and exiles on the earth." These commendable, exemplary heroes of the faith made the list not because they received everything they hoped for but rather because they didn't. They simply held on.

Life didn't turn out the way they had imagined. They didn't get the deliverance. They didn't get the "blessing." All they got was the promise of "a better country, that is, a heavenly one" (verse 16), and they died before they saw it ultimately fulfilled.

Yet they endured. They didn't know the plan as we know it now—that God's promise of an eternal inheritance would be made perfect through the sacrifice of Jesus Christ for the sins of the world. They could not imagine that Jesus's *even if* obedience would secure our futures and fulfill all God's promises.

"Therefore," the explanation continues, "since we are surrounded by so great a cloud of witnesses, let us also lay aside every weight, and sin which clings so closely, and let us run with endurance the race that is set before us, looking to Jesus, the founder and perfecter of our faith" (12:1–2).

There's a play on words here in the original Greek text that gets lost in translation. Literally the writer said, "Since we have *set around* us a great cloud of witnesses . . . let us run with endurance the race that is *set before* us." The example is set around us. We have set around us the testimonies of faithful heroes who didn't receive what was promised them yet held on to their faith by enduring. It's as if the writer were saying, "Countless *even if* runners went before us and are around us, so run the race set before you."

Everyone has a race to run, a race with unique obstacles. Each of us has unique burdens and sins that entangle us and threaten to trip us up. We each have *only if*s, *if only*s, and *what if*s that burden us, paralyze us, and keep us from running. As a result, we have unique *even if* lives to live. But that doesn't mean that we're alone. Uniqueness doesn't mean isolation.

The beautiful promise of Hebrews 11 is that lives filled with all sorts of unexpected turns don't disqualify us from the community of faith. Hardships and disappointments don't mean that somehow our faith is inadequate. Rather, by that very measure, we are counted in the Hall of Faith, surrounded by *even if* witnesses who call us to endure and resolve to worship God.

We could look at example after example of suffering, bewildered, disappointed, yet hopeful, faith-filled *even if* heroes who chose to worship God in the midst of the fire.

MODERN-DAY WITNESSES

Pay attention, and you'll see modern-day *even if* witnesses too. TobyMac, the ever-enduring, seemingly ageless performer, tragically lost his son to an accidental overdose. I had the opportunity to serve with him at a youth camp he sponsored for young athletes through the Fellowship of Christian Athletes. I knew then that he was the real deal—he loved the Lord and loved people.

The day after his son's passing, he posted, "My wife and I would want the world to know this . . . We don't follow God because we have some sort of under-the-table deal with Him, like, we'll follow you if you bless us. We follow God because we love Him. It's our honor. He is the God of the hills and the valleys. And He is beautiful above all things."[4] *Even if.*

I've sat with *even if* witnesses just days before either of us knew that cancer would be their ticket home. They worshipped God with literally the last breath in their lungs. I've encountered *even if* witnesses as they've shared with me their God-sized dreams, asking me to pray with them as they nervously take the next steps of obedience.

I've walked with *even if* witnesses courageously living out their singleness with both longing and purpose. While they name the desire to be married, they hold it with an open hand, declaring *even if* . . . they will worship the Lord and serve his purposes.

My dear friend Elizabeth, who is known at our church as "the pie lady" because of her blue-ribbon-winning spiritual gift of making heavenly apple pies, is also an *even if* warrior. Growing up devoutly Mormon, Elizabeth had to weigh the cost of surrendering to Jesus and being subsequently disowned by her family.

"*Even if* I walk alone in this world, I will follow the Lord."

When she met the man she wanted to marry, her parents were openly opposed. She knew that God wanted them to honor their parents and wait for their blessing. They chose to wait on the Lord and surrender their desires to his timing. They waited six years.

"*Even if* we have to remain single forever, we will worship the Lord."

They desperately wanted to have a family. It took longer than they had hoped to conceive. And then they lost their first baby to a miscarriage.

"*Even if* we can't have children, we will worship the Lord." They had a son and then another miscarriage. And then five more children.

Then Elizabeth was diagnosed with cancer. Hadn't she already demonstrated her faith? Each doctor's appointment required another level of trust as her diagnosis kept getting worse. Chemotherapy ravaged her body.

"*Even if* I don't survive, I will worship the Lord."

She recovered from cancer in time to become a caregiver to her mother, whose mind was lost to Alzheimer's disease. There were many dark days when her mother would lash out at her like a hostile stranger.

"*Even if* my own mother doesn't know me, I will worship the Lord." She had the privilege of being with her to the end.

As she shared the chapters of her *even if* life, Elizabeth tearfully and gratefully summed it up: "These trials or situations have not caused my faith to waver but have been the foundation and cornerstones of faith that have given me confidence to walk boldly in the face of trials. As earth-shattering as they may have been, they have made my God-confidence more secure."

All these witnesses have encouraged, strengthened, and humbled me, but none more so than the *even if* witness who lives with

me, my wife. At the time of writing this, I am watching my beloved bride make her own *even if* declaration as she grieves the
loss of her mother to breast cancer.

Mother-in-law jokes are lost on me. The punch lines about
pushy, overbearing meddlers are way outside my own experience.
My mother-in-law was an incredible woman who loved me deeply.
After immigrating here from South Korea, she relearned a nursing profession from which she would retire forty-two years later
and tirelessly cared for not just our family but our extended circle
of aunts and uncles.

She always ate last; most of her own meals were lukewarm and
consisted of the remaining portions after everyone else had been
served. Like a spy passing on secrets, she would clandestinely slip
our kids little gifts of spending money when no one was looking.
She was a master at finding bargains, but whenever she went
shopping for deals, she would return with shopping bags of
clothes . . . for her grandkids. No one deserves to get cancer, especially not her.

As her suffering and pain increased, I witnessed my wife wrestling with so many *counter if*s. She prayed for healing and faced
many frustrations and disappointments as the cancer progressed.
Especially in the last month of her mother's life, she wrestled
with the question, *Why does God continue to let her suffer?* "If he
is not going to heal her, why doesn't he take her to be home with
him?"

Together, we learned to name each complaint, speak what was
in our hearts, and lay it before the Lord. Neither of us freaked
out, though we did ugly cry at times. We did not rebuke each
other when speaking our sadness and complaints. We voiced our
great anger over cancer and the state of our world. Our heartache
poured out in numbing silence as well as guttural sobs.

We worked through many contingencies related to her mom's
passing. *What if* she never gets to see her grandkids graduate?

Get married? *What if* she passes before Thanksgiving? *What if* she sticks around until next year? With each question, we released our control over the matter and looked to the sovereign One, who had been good to us thus far. We declared, "*Even if* you take our beloved mother, we will trust you and worship you. You've blessed us with her life for these years. We are sad and hurting, but we are grateful."

After a yearlong battle, she left us on Christmas morning. It's fitting that she left us to be with the Lord on the day we traditionally celebrate God's coming to us. Her longing was to go home, and she had prepared both domestically (by giving away most of her stuff) and relationally (by having the conversations she needed to have).

Even after her passing, regrets needed to be wrestled with. *If only* we had done some other treatment. *If only* she were around for another year. *If only* we had taken her to hospice earlier or later. Did we do everything we could have? Did we do right by her? We are still in the midst of working this out, even as new regrets arise from the COVID-19 reality we are living through. We're sure that there will be new conditions and contingencies that our new "normal" will reveal and, most importantly, new opportunities to declare *even if.*

The collective testimony of these witnesses reminds me that the *even if* declaration isn't a one-time banner you raise. It's a tapestry that is woven through the working out of persevering faith in real time, along the ups and downs of the journey. Each new challenge brings a new opportunity to remember God's goodness and to resolve to worship him. What you are experiencing, while unique to you, is not foreign to the collective experience of God's people.

No matter how your journey unfolds from this point forward, remember that we're not alone. When we declare our *even if,* you and I are standing on the shoulders of *even if* saints, who trusted

God in the midst of great disappointment and hardship. You and I are surrounded by a family of *even if* witnesses—both ancient and modern—to remind us that the *even if* life isn't for naught.

Do you have a more immediate *even if* community as well? If not, whom could you invite to journey with you? You don't have to have the same struggles. You don't even need to be in the same season or leg of the journey. You just need to share an *even if* faith that trusts in God's goodness. You could share your *even if* declaration with a few people. As you take your next step, you can invite a few friends to support you in it. You can ask what steps your friends are taking. There are practical ways to live out an *even if* life together. You don't have to go alone.

SHEPHERDING FROM THE BACK

While your *even if* journey might be different from mine, remember that ultimately we are all in the hands of the same good God—the One who will meet us and provide for us just as he has for his people for generations.

Don't overlook that point. God is with us. He is not distant. He is near and involved. The iconic psalm reminds us,

> The LORD is my shepherd; I shall not want.
> He makes me lie down in green pastures.
> He leads me beside still waters. . . .
> Even though I walk through the valley of the shadow of
>   death,
>   I will fear no evil,
> for you are with me. (23:1–2, 4)

No matter how dark the valley might seem, God is with us. Therefore, we will not fear.

Though foreign to our modern lifestyles, the picture of God as a shepherd is still a comforting one. It's why Psalm 23 is often read at the bedside of a sick patient or at a funeral. We imagine ourselves as his sheep in the midst of a threatening wilderness. God, as our shepherd, provides for, guides, and protects us in the valley of the shadow of death. Everyone longs for protection, guidance, and the safety that follows.

Have you ever stopped to consider *how* God shepherds his flock? Maybe it's the influence of paintings I saw growing up, but when I imagined a shepherd leading his flock, I pictured the shepherd, staff in hand, with the sheep following neatly behind. Of course, the shepherd also had a flowing white robe and hair that looked like it was straight out of a shampoo commercial. The idyllic picture gave that warm feeling of a shepherd tending his sheep.

A few years ago, I was traveling through the wilderness of Israel when I realized how off my imagination was. I stumbled upon a huge flock of hundreds of sheep and goats being led through the Judean wilderness. The flock spread out over the hillside like the shadow of a cloud. It wasn't an orderly following as much as it was a sprawling mass. At first, I couldn't tell which was the front or the back. More concerningly, I couldn't see the shepherd. I scanned the flock as it crept along. There was no one at the helm.

That's when I saw him. At first, I missed the shepherd because I was looking in the wrong place. He wasn't at the front of the flock. He was at the back, driving the herd with just his voice and the help of a few sheep hands and dogs. The picture puzzled me, but the more I thought about it, the more it made sense. The shepherd doesn't usually lead his flock from the front. How can a shepherd protect his flock if his back is to them? How will he know if a predator is coming or if a member is lagging behind? The ideal vantage point is at the back, behind the sheep. He can see all the potential dangers as well as the road ahead.

Here's the tension, though: what is safest for the sheep is also most unnerving. The sheep can't see the shepherd. They can only hear his voice. They take each step, trusting in the care and protection of the shepherd who is watching over them. While they might be in his sights, the shepherd is not in theirs.

While actual sheep might be okay with that, it's a lot harder to swallow when the metaphor is applied to our relationships with God. What happens when we can't see the Shepherd in front of us? Fear begins to set in. Maybe even a little paralysis. We question where we are and where we are going. Even as we proceed, we feel uncertain and a bit clumsy.

PUT YOUR HANDS WHERE I CAN SEE THEM

I experienced this the first time my little girl rode a two-wheel bike on her own. It was a proud but fearful moment. While I was astonished at her ability—she was years ahead of when her brothers first rode—I was also terrified that she would crash into the pavement. Her feet couldn't quite reach the ground because she was on her older brother's bike. She felt unsteady turning the handlebars at just the right angle so as not to come to a violent halt. So she begged me to run alongside her as she pedaled, demanding that I hold the handlebar as she sped along.

At first, I gladly obliged. It was a bit of reassurance for me and for her mother that Daddy would make sure she was safe. Pretty soon she began riding faster, and I could barely keep up. As I held on to the handle, it would cause her to swerve toward me, a dangerous situation for her and for me. I ended up putting my hand on her back in order to steady her. Though I was giving her the same support and even better balance, it wasn't enough for her. She grew reticent and fearful.

"Put your hands on the handle, Daddy!" she cried in fear.

"Honey, Daddy's hand is on your back. That way, you won't

swerve to one side. I've got you," I assured her, gasping for breath
in full stride alongside her.

"No, Daddy, put your hands where I can see them!"

That's all that mattered to her. It wasn't enough for her that she
could feel my steadying hand on her back. It wasn't enough that
our new configuration allowed her to ride smoother. It wasn't
even enough that I was still running right alongside. She needed
to see my hands. She wanted me to shepherd her from the front.

Do we often demand that of God as our shepherd? To be led
from the front? "Put your hands where we can see them, God."
We want his goodness to be predictable. We believe that there's
more comfort and protection when we can understand what he is
doing. We have trouble believing that he is at work when the
shadow of the valley or the blinding heat of the furnace causes his
hands to fade from sight.

But that doesn't mean he isn't at work. The good Shepherd is
leading you and protecting you. He always has, and he won't stop
now. The latest challenge you're facing isn't a sign that he has
abandoned you. The next hardship you encounter won't mean
that he has forgotten you. It's just that, like a good shepherd, he
might be leading you from behind.

This isn't just a principle plucked from Psalm 23. Even in the
book of Isaiah, the prophet comforted God's people that as they
walked through hardship, even as a result of their own sin, God
would show them mercy: "Your ears shall hear a word behind
you, saying, 'This is the way, walk in it,' when you turn to the right
or when you turn to the left" (30:21). God will remain faithful to
lead us even when we are not faithful to him.

That means you can know God's voice and his presence *even if*
you can't see his hands at the moment. He might not come as a
pillar of fire or cloud leading you through your wilderness. With
his shepherding, you won't necessarily avoid the valley. But know
that he is your shepherd, and remember that shepherds often

lead from the rear. He sees you. He knows your fears. He sees the landscape ahead even better than you do.

You might think that because his hands are not on the handlebar, maybe he's just left you to struggle through the tough terrain you're going through right now. That's not the God of the Bible, the God who allowed his very own Son to go through the worst valley imaginable—death on a cross. All so that you and I could be called his children, so that we could be called the sheep of his hand. If God went to such lengths to save us, adopt us, and give us new life, he's not going to abandon us now.

Romans 8:32 reminds us, "He who did not spare his own Son but gave him up for us all, how will he not also with him graciously give us all things?" "All things" includes guidance. Protection comes with it too. It even includes the strength to endure. Like a Father holding the seat of your bike, he has his hands on your life. His goodness hasn't run out. He is with you, watching over you, even running alongside you. How can you know that for sure?

The very fact that you're reading this means you're here. I know that's incredibly obvious, but hang with me for a moment. One of the most profound bits of counsel I have received is the simple observation that wherever you are, there you are. No matter how hard life is, you have made it thus far. You are here. Alive. Hanging on. You haven't thrown in the towel, even if you wanted to. No matter how dark life might seem or how unsettling it actually is, you are not where you were. Even if it's been a year you want to forget, consider that you made it through if only by the barest thread of faith.

How did you get here? Did you get here on your own?

No, a good Shepherd has been walking with you and guiding you. Even if you couldn't always see him, you are here because of his mercy, and he won't fail you now. You may not like how you arrived, but God has great compassion for you. He desires to lead you to greener pastures and stiller waters. He won't abandon you in the valley. And as he leads you, he will ask you to trust him by taking a risk. He will ask you to take the next step *even if* you can't see where the path leads.

He will call you to lay aside the conditions you hold on to, those conditions that express your will, not his. He'll challenge you to lay down your regrets and live in the reality of one who is beloved, warts and all. He'll ask you to exchange your contingency plans for his will, a will that won't always be revealed in the amount of detail you want. The Shepherd does all that and more out of his love for you.

No matter what your journey may bring, the Shepherd of your soul will be good to you just as he has been good to those who have gone before you and those who surround you even now. The Cross guarantees it. The cloud of witnesses testify to it. The *even if* declaration of your heart will be lived out of it.

As God does all this in your life, you will experience the depths of his presence, of knowing and loving a God whose goodness isn't contingent on what leg of the journey you happen to be on. You will know his tenderness in a hospital room. You will sense his care and friendship when you are all alone. When tragedy strikes, when disappointments come, when unexpected twists and turns pull you here and there, your way forward will be found in remembering that God is with you, and you'll declare *even if.*

To say *even if* is to declare that you will trust in the Shepherd, who's always trustworthy. He gives you peace when none should be reasonably found and contentment even when the situation is not what you had hoped for. It's to say that you trust in the One whom you can't always see, because you know he won't leave you or forsake you. You are his, and therefore, your story will be counted among the *even if* cloud of witnesses, grafted ultimately into *the* story of God's love for the world.

As you run the race set before you, may God write new stanzas of your *even if* declaration, accumulating them for the day when they will be recited in the company of all the *even if* witnesses set around us. On that day, we will know that our struggles weren't in vain and that our faith in God was more than just "cross your fingers" optimism. When he reveals the work that he did through us and in us all along the way, we will know that we were sustained by a good God who is even more good to us than we imagined at first. Until then, with every hardship and every blessing, declare his goodness *even if*.

EVEN IF PREAYERS FOR YOU

For much of my prayer life, I believed that God preferred extemporaneous, unique prayers. Prayer books and recited prayers felt inauthentic to me, and I assumed that God frowned on them. I have since come to really appreciate prayers that others have written, both for their depth of insight and for their sheer helpfulness.

When I don't have the words, I have found that prayers written by others can help give voice to the deeper things in my heart. They expand my prayer language, inviting me to pray about matters that either escape my attention or feel off-limits for one reason or another. They remind me that God hears the sincerity of my heart, not the originality of my words.

I would now like to offer some prayers to you—prayers that I have written that you can pray for yourself or share with others. You can pray them aloud word for word, or you can paraphrase them into your own utterances. You could begin in one prayer and end up praying something different altogether. These prayers are just starting points into deeper intimacy with the God who hears and knows you. My hope is that they help give voice to a whole new volume of *even if* prayers uniquely spoken by you.

AN *EVEN IF* PRAYER FOR WHEN YOU FEEL STUCK

O God who sees me,

You know my heart and desires.
You know all my strivings and attempts.
I thought I would be further along.
The rut I'm in feels inescapable.

Father, I feel this pressure to keep up, to be better.
I see all around what people are achieving,
New chapters that are opening for them,
And I feel like the world is moving on without me.

Guard me from comparisons, Lord—
From seeing where others are and what they have received.
Remind me that not all is ever as it seems.
Assure me that I am right where you want me to be
And that your intentions for me are good.

You have not forgotten me.
I haven't slipped through the cracks of your mercy and compassion.
In this season of restlessness, when things are not the way I want them to be,
Help me find my contentment in you,
The One who knows what I need even better than I do.

Even if my life lags behind the lives of those around me,
I remember that you came to give me life, life to the full.
Even if I can't see a way forward,
I trust that you, Jesus, are the way, the truth, and the life.
I will wait on you, God, for you are never late.
Amen.

AN *EVEN IF* PRAYER FOR WHEN YOU ARE DISAPPOINTED

Father,

This is not the way it was supposed to go.
I believed you for a different outcome.
Deep down, I was hoping for something else.
Like the dreams of the disciples who thought Jesus would
    come down from that cross
But instead saw him laid in a tomb,
My dreams feel dashed.

In your goodness, attend to my disappointment as a com-
    passionate Father.
Be patient with my limited understanding.
If my expectations were unrealistic, gently correct me.
If I'm not seeing the whole picture, give me a glimpse of
    what I'm missing.

I ask you this, not as a jury that demands satisfaction
But as your child who trusts your goodness enough
To feel the disappointment when you don't do what I know
    you could.
Restrain my imagination in ways that are beneficial.
Stretch my assumptions in ways that lead to hope.

I know that you are at work even in this.
Disappointments lose their grip in the light of an empty tomb
That no one could have anticipated.
There's no obstacle too big for you.

Even if I can't see what you're doing,
Even if it's different from what I wanted,
I believe that you bring life from death,
Resurrected dreams from dashed hopes.

Turn this mourning into dancing.
Bring beauty from these ashes.
I've seen you do it time and time again.
I will wait for you.
Amen.

AN *EVEN IF* PRAYER FOR WHEN YOU FAIL

God of second chances,

I'm in need of your mercy anew today.
I gave it my best shot but still came up short.
You know my intentions were good,
Even though the expression missed the mark.

I am sorry I couldn't be stronger, wiser, and godlier.
Yet my inadequacy is no surprise to you.
You remember that I am but dust,
Even as I forget it all too often.

Quiet the voices of self-condemnation.
Remind me that I am more than the sum of my mistakes,
That my worth comes from more than what I can accomplish.

Do not let my desire for approval define my response in the
   aftermath.

Lift up my head, Father; remove from me my shame.
Grant me the courage to look honestly at my failure
And to learn what you intend to show me through it.
By your kindness, help me take the next steps required.

I thank you that there is no failure great enough
To separate me from your love.
I can face the music of my mistakes
Because there is no condemnation for those in Christ Jesus.

Even if my failure follows closely behind
Or always seems to stay one step ahead of me,
Even if my attempts to course correct are not received,

I will remember that with you there is forgiveness,
That Jesus's victory overcomes my failures.
I will remember that I have no reputation to defend,
Because the only reputation worth having is the one you be-
   stow on me,
The reputation that comes by grace through faith,
The high calling of being your beloved.
Amen.

AN *EVEN IF* PRAYER BEFORE YOU TAKE A RISK

God of glory,

I can't deny the passion you've put in my heart.
Like a fire shut up in my bones, the need to step out stirs me.
Yet I am fearful.

The questions of *What if?* rule my heart.
The need for success only adds to the pressure.

I confess my fear of uncertainty.
I am too attached to my résumé.
I would rather play it safe
And keep to the status quo.

But you won't let me.
You saved me not for comfort but for a calling.
You have opened my eyes to a new possibility for life,
A life marked by love, justice, and righteousness.
I cannot unsee the world-changing potential of your king-
dom cause.

I don't know how this risk will turn out.
But I know who you are.
I know that you are worthy
And that you are the one committed to advancing your king-
dom.

You know that my heart's desire is to bring you the glory you
deserve.
I know your power and ability to bring it about.
So I surrender my reputation to you.
I lay down my need for success.

Grant me the courage to do what needs to be done.
Steady me as I step out of the boat into turbulent waters.
Protect me, and may yours be to me the only opinion that
truly matters.
Guard me from defensiveness when the inevitable critiques
come.

Even if this risk does not pan out,
Even if it brings pain and discomfort,
You are worthy of my best efforts.
So I leave the results of my obedience to you.
For I know that come success or failure,
I am yours, and nothing can change that.
Amen.

AN *EVEN IF* PRAYER WHEN YOUR PAST COMES HAUNTING

God of new beginnings,

Where would I be today without the intervention of your
    grace?
You opened my ears to hear your voice,
Called me from death to life.
You rescued me from myself and gave me a new identity as
    your child.

Yet the burden of my past and the memories of my former
    life plague me.
They tell me who I was and whisper that I will never be any-
    thing different.
I painfully remember the ways I defied you
When I was hell-bent on being my own god.
If only I could undo my past!
If only I had known your tender mercy sooner.

Still, this I call to mind:
Your timing is perfect;
Your plan is intentional.
There are no wasted years in your kingdom.

Though I wish I could make up for time lost,
I remember that your goodness to me is more than I de-
    serve.
You remove my sins far from me,
As far as east is from west.
You remember them no more.

Help me live in the newness of how you define me:
As your child, not as an enemy,
As your friend, not as a rebel,
As your beloved, not as a debtor.

Even if I cannot undo my past,
Even if I can never repay you,
I fall on the mercy of my Savior
And believe that what he has done for me is enough.

I worship you for your ability to make all things new,
Beginning with my heart even unto the end of the age.
Amen.

ACKNOWLEDGMENTS

My dear bride, Sarah: Thanks for being my cheerleader and chief encourager when I didn't think I could do this. You gave me permission to disappear in order to write, taking on more than your fair share of duties to keep our kiddos from burning down the house or killing one another. Who would have thought that when we parted ways in that parking lot so many years ago, we would live to write about it? You and me, babe. *Even if.*

My tribe—Calvin, Noah, Ben, Beatrice, and Owen: How is it that the source of so much insanity in my life has actually kept me sane? Our life together is the canvas on which God has lovingly exposed my conditions, regrets, and contingency plans. Thanks for being so excited about the book and fighting over who would be mentioned more. Dad loves you . . . no matter what . . . always . . . forever . . . this much . . . *even if.*

My dad, Edward, and my mother-in-law, Kyung: I wish you could have held this book in your hands. Your lives helped write it.

My mom, Susie: Walking through the loss of Dad has been one of the hardest *even if* seasons of our lives. Yet worshipping God in the midst of it—and continuing to do so—has only added to your *even if* lore. Thanks for being so committed to me and my ministry.

My *bobae,* Sylvia: You could have written this book faster and with far more depth of insight. Thanks for sharing in my joy by being a sounding board for ideas, adding color to points, and being even more excited about this project than I was at times. Your enthusiasm and pride over it got me unstuck more times than you know.

My Grace Community Church family: Your enthusiasm for this project overflows from a sincere faith and sweet disposition that every pastor should get to experience. Your desire to please God makes me want to be the kind of pastor you deserve.

Thanks also to my brothers-in-arms, the fellow elders of Grace, for encouraging me, giving me the margin to write, and wisely helping me discern how to steward this message well.

My agent, Don: Your inquiry after a simple message in James was the spark that finally got me to say, "Yes, Lord." Thanks for processing through my fears as an agenda-free listener and being a willing reader, encourager, and champion.

Susan: I still can't believe you took a chance on me. I am grateful for your insightful comments, your tender treatment of this fledgling author's ego, and your enduring belief that this message could help people. Thanks to you and the team.

Diane: Thank you for playing fact-checker, source compiler, context scanner, first reviewer . . . all while keeping my life and ministry organized! Your ministry alongside me reminds me that God gives us exactly what we need. You, indeed, are a gift to me.

Forrest and Kara: Your struggle through loss and grief and your commitment to worship God in the midst of it all demonstrate the power and beauty of the *even if* life. Thanks for entrusting me with your story.

Ian and "the pastors": Thanks for helping me think through

and wordsmith the clunky parts of this book. Ian, chapter 4 wouldn't have been written without you. Matt, I think I would have given up before I even wrote a word were it not for you. Kelsey, thanks for encouraging my voice. Our Zoom chats, bourbon bonfires, Deep Creek adventures, and conversations around pastoral ministry and life are what every pastor needs and deserves.

Jimmy, John, and "the fellowship of the fish": You knew exactly when to leave me alone to write, when to entice me to jump into a river in order to clear my head, and when to celebrate with me after a deadline. Such discernment comes only over many brown trout giggles and bag nights. I am grateful for the renewed vigor and perspective each of our encounters provided me. Tight lines.

Community Fellowship Church: Our eight years together were the whiteboard on which the *even if* formula was worked out. I will forever be indebted to you for the way you demonstrated the gospel to me and my new bride, taking us in as newlyweds and sending us out as adults.

Elizabeth, Chad, Toni, Dave and Erin, Will and Naomi, Leslie, and Betty: your stories illustrate the *even if* life and give me strength to live out my own.

The Pioneers family all over the world: You are my *even if* heroes—declaring, enduring, resolving, and sacrificing in order to see the fame of Jesus demonstrated in churches among the most unreached. It's one thing to declare it. You live it.

The countless *even if* witnesses whose lives imprinted this book: Your stories are the essential threads of the beautiful *even if* tapestry God is weaving. The fact that you are simply living out your *even if* declarations with no need for fanfare declares the goodness of God on so many levels.

NOTES

WELCOME TO THE VALLEY

1. David Brooks, *The Second Mountain: The Quest for a Moral Life* (New York: Random House, 2019), xvi.

PART 1: SOMEWHERE BEYOND THE SEA

1. "Breakpoint: Dunkirk, 'And If Not,' " Breakpoint, August 4, 2017, www .breakpoint.org/breakpoint-dunkirk-and-if-not.
2. Walter Lord, *The Miracle of Dunkirk: The True Story of Operation Dynamo* (New York: Open Road, 2017).
3. Martin Luther King Jr., "I Have a Dream," speech, March on Washington, August 28, 1963, Washington, DC, The Martin Luther King, Jr. Research and Education Institute, https://kinginstitute.stanford.edu/ king-papers/documents/i-have-dream-address-delivered-march-washington -jobs-and-freedom.

CHAPTER 1: OUT OF THE FIRE . . . OR INTO IT?

1. David Brooks, *The Second Mountain: The Quest for a Moral Life* (New York: Random House, 2019), 212.
2. Fleming Rutledge, *Advent: The Once and Future Coming of Jesus Christ* (Grand Rapids, MI: Eerdmans, 2018), 330.
3. Timothy Keller, *Walking with God Through Pain and Suffering* (New York: Riverhead Books, 2015), 230–31.

CHAPTER 2: GOODNESS IN THE DEEP END OF THE POOL

1. A. W. Tozer, *The Knowledge of the Holy* (New York: HarperOne, 1961), 1.
2. C. S. Lewis, *The Lion, the Witch and the Wardrobe* (London: HarperCollins Children's Books, 2015), 75.
3. Cornelius Plantinga Jr., quoting Dale Cooper, *Reading for Preaching: The Preacher in Conversation with Storytellers, Biographers, Poets, and Journalists* (Grand Rapids, MI: Eerdmans, 2013), 96.
4. I am grateful for the influence of Paul David Tripp, *Awe: Why It Matters for Everything We Think, Say, and Do* (Wheaton, IL: Crossway, 2015), 115–16.
5. Neil Postman, *Amusing Ourselves to Death: Public Discourse in the Age of Show Business* (New York: Penguin Books, 2006), 99–100.
6. Gerard Manley Hopkins, "God's Grandeur," in *The Major Works,* ed. Catherine Phillips (Oxford: Oxford University Press, 2009), 128.
7. Harold Sevener, ed., *Messianic Passover Haggadah* (New York: Chosen People Ministries, 2000), 21–25.
8. J. I. Packer, *Knowing God* (Downers Grove, IL: IVP Books, 2018), 23.

CHAPTER 3: MORE THAN A NEW YEAR'S RESOLUTION

1. Kate Bowler, *Everything Happens for a Reason: And Other Lies I've Loved* (New York: Random House, 2018), 106–25.
2. D. Martyn Lloyd-Jones, *Spiritual Depression: Its Causes and Its Cure* (Grand Rapids, MI: Eerdmans, 1965), 20.
3. *Religious Affections,* ed. John E. Smith, vol. 2, *The Works of Jonathan Edwards,* ed. Perry Miller (New Haven, CT: Yale University Press, 1959), 240–53.
4. C. S. Lewis, *Surprised by Joy: The Shape of My Early Life* (New York: Harcourt Brace Jovanovich, 1955), 77.

CHAPTER 4: I WANT IT MY WAY

1. I'm so grateful for the work of Paul David Tripp in helping me see this progression in my heart. Paul David Tripp, *Instruments in the Redeemer's Hands: People in Need of Change Helping People in Need of Change* (Phillipsburg, NJ: P&R, 2002), 87–88.
2. C. S. Lewis, *Mere Christianity* (New York: HarperOne, 2001), 136–37.
3. Eugene H. Peterson, *Five Smooth Stones for Pastoral Work* (Grand Rapids, MI: Eerdmans, 1992), 176.

4. William Clark, *The Glorious Mess: Who We Are and How We Relate* (Reston, VA: Lay Counselor Institute, 2010–12).
5. Timothy Keller, *The Meaning of Marriage* (New York: Riverhead Books, 2011), 44.
6. Heather Davis Nelson, *Unashamed: Healing Our Brokenness and Finding Freedom from Shame* (Wheaton, IL: Crossway, 2016), 89–91.
7. Philip Yancey, *Reaching for the Invisible God: What Can We Expect to Find?* (Grand Rapids, MI: Zondervan, 2000), 69.
8. Pete Greig, *How to Pray: A Simple Guide for Normal People* (Colorado Springs, CO: NavPress, 2019), 57.
9. George Everett Ross, quoted in Yancey, *Reaching,* 52–53.

CHAPTER 5: FAKE IT TILL YOU MAKE IT

1. *Sliding Doors,* directed by Peter Howitt, Intermedia Films, 1998.
2. Philip Seymour Hoffman, quoted in "Philip Seymour Hoffman: Broadway's New 'Salesman,'" NPR, April 12, 2012, www.npr.org/2012/04/12/150305122/philip-seymour-hoffman-broadways-new-salesman.
3. Brené Brown, *Daring Greatly: How the Courage to Be Vulnerable Transforms the Way We Live, Love, Parent, and Lead* (New York: Gotham Books, 2012), 26.
4. John Newton, "Amazing Grace," 1779, public domain.
5. Bryan Stevenson, *Just Mercy: A Story of Justice and Redemption* (New York: Spiegel & Grau, 2014), 290.
6. Jon Bloom, "If Only," Desiring God, October 27, 2017, www.desiringgod.org/articles/if-only.
7. Charlie Mackesy, *The Boy, the Mole, the Fox and the Horse* (New York: HarperOne, 2019), 12.
8. Brennan Manning, *Abba's Child: The Cry of the Heart for Intimate Belonging* (Colorado Springs, CO: NavPress, 2015), 15–30.
9. Mark Buchanan, *Spiritual Rhythm: Being with Jesus Every Season of Your Soul* (Grand Rapids, MI: Zondervan, 2010), 53.
10. Thomas Merton, *New Seeds of Contemplation* (New York: New Directions, 2007), 34.

CHAPTER 6: CONTROL FREAKS OF THE WORLD . . . UNITE
(IN CAREFULLY THOUGHT-OUT, APPROPRIATE WAYS)

1. Max Lucado, *Anxious for Nothing: Finding Calm in a Chaotic World* (Nashville, TN: Thomas Nelson, 2017), 3–4.

2. Lucado, *Anxious for Nothing*, 24.
3. Sheldon Vanauken, *A Severe Mercy* (New York: Harper & Row, 1987), 27.
4. Vanauken, *A Severe Mercy*, 35.
5. Vanauken, *A Severe Mercy*, 216.

CHAPTER 7: IT STARTS HERE

1. James K. A. Smith, *You Are What You Love: The Spiritual Power of Habit* (Grand Rapids, MI: Brazos, 2016), 11.
2. Smith, *You Are What You Love*, 37.
3. Fred Rogers, "Fred Rogers Acceptance Speech," Daytime Emmy Awards, Radio City Music Hall, May 21, 1997, New York, YouTube, www.youtube.com/watch?v=Upm9LnuCBUM.
4. Max Lucado, *Anxious for Nothing: Finding Calm in a Chaotic World* (Nashville, TN: Thomas Nelson, 2017), 94.
5. Jack Deere, *Even in Our Darkness: A Story of Beauty in a Broken Life* (Grand Rapids, MI: Zondervan, 2018), 203.
6. Miroslav Volf, *Free of Charge: Giving and Forgiving in a Culture Stripped of Grace* (Grand Rapids, MI: Zondervan, 2005), 108–10.
7. J. I. Packer, *Knowing God* (Downers Grove, IL: IVP Books, 2018), 30–31.

CHAPTER 8: PERMISSION TO SPEAK FREELY

1. Brian Stone, "Fully Alive: God's Dream for Us," in *Learning Change: Congregational Transformation Fueled by Personal Renewal*, ed. Jim Herrington and Trisha Taylor (Grand Rapids, MI: Kregel Ministry, 2017), 21.
2. Mark Buchanan, *Spiritual Rhythm: Being with Jesus Every Season of Your Soul* (Grand Rapids, MI: Zondervan, 2010), 46.
3. Aubrey Sampson, *The Louder Song: Listening for Hope in the Midst of Lament* (Colorado Springs, CO: NavPress, 2019), 111–14.
4. Sampson, *The Louder Song*, 113.
5. Jen Pollock Michel, *Surprised by Paradox: The Promise of And in an Either-Or World* (Downers Grove, IL: IVP Books, 2019), 163.

CHAPTER 9: RISK-TAKERS, DAREDEVILS, AND OTHER PEOPLE WHO MAKE ME NERVOUS

1. Martin Luther, "A Mighty Fortress Is Our God," trans. Frederick H. Hedge, 1852, public domain.

2. John Piper, *Risk Is Right: Better to Lose Your Life Than to Waste It* (Wheaton, IL: Crossway, 2013), 17.
3. Karen Swallow Prior, *On Reading Well: Finding the Good Life Through Great Books* (Grand Rapids, MI: Brazos, 2018), 94.
4. Chip Heath and Dan Heath, *The Power of Moments: Why Certain Experiences Have Extraordinary Impact* (New York: Simon & Schuster, 2017), 113–31.
5. Heath and Heath, *The Power of Moments*, 131.
6. Heath and Heath, *The Power of Moments*, 131.
7. Ed Catmull, *Creativity, Inc.: Overcoming the Unseen Forces That Stand in the Way of True Inspiration* (New York: Random House, 2014), 279–81.
8. Catmull, *Creativity, Inc.*, 114.
9. Mark Batterson, "The Lion Chaser's Manifesto," in *Chase the Lion: If Your Dream Doesn't Scare You, It's Too Small* (Colorado Springs, CO: Multnomah, 2019).
10. Justin Whitmel Earley, *The Common Rule: Habits of Purpose for an Age of Distraction* (Downers Grove, IL: IVP Books, 2019), 162.
11. Philip Yancey, *Reaching for the Invisible God: What Can We Expect to Find?* (Grand Rapids, MI: Zondervan, 2000), 47.
12. C. S. Lewis, *The Screwtape Letters* (San Francisco: HarperSanFrancisco, 2001), 60.
13. Charlie Mackesy, *The Boy, the Mole, the Fox and the Horse* (New York: HarperOne, 2019), 67.

CHAPTER 10: TAKE A STEP (BUT NOT BY YOURSELF)

1. Henri Nouwen, quoted in Michael J. Christensen, "Henri Nouwen on Hearing a Deeper Beat," in Henri Nouwen, *Discernment: Reading the Signs of Daily Life* (New York: HarperOne, 2013), 179.
2. Joseph Campbell, quoted in Brené Brown, *Braving the Wilderness: The Quest for True Belonging and the Courage to Stand Alone* (New York: Random House, 2017), 40.
3. Author unknown. Quoted in Justin Taylor, "Do the Next Thing," The Gospel Coalition, October 25, 2017, www.thegospelcoalition.org/blogs/justin-taylor/do-the-next-thing.
4. TobyMac, Facebook, October 24, 2019, www.facebook.com/tobymac/posts/10156560898076179.